# UNIVERSAL GRAMMAR
## IN CHILD SECOND LANGUAGE ACQUISITION
### NULL SUBJECTS AND MORPHOLOGICAL UNIFORMITY

# LANGUAGE ACQUISITION & LANGUAGE DISORDERS

### EDITORS

Harald Clahsen  William Rutherford
*University of Essex*  *University of Southern California*

### EDITORIAL BOARD

Melissa Bowerman (Max Planck Institut für Psycholinguistik, Nijmegen)
Patricia Clancy (University of California at Santa Barbara)
Werner Deutsch (Universität Braunschweig)
Kenji Hakuta (Stanford University)
Kenneth Hyltenstam (University of Stockholm)
Peter Jordens (Free University, Amsterdam)
Barry McLaughlin (University of California at Santa Cruz)
Jürgen Meisel (Universität Hamburg)
Anne Mills (University of Amsterdam)
Csaba Pleh (University of Budapest)
Michael Sharwood Smith (University of Utrecht)
Catherine Snow (Harvard University)
Jürgen Weissenborn (Max Planck Institut für Psycholinguistik, Nijmegen)
Lydia White (McGill University)
Helmut Zobl (Carleton University, Ottawa)

Volume 10

Usha Lakshmanan

*Universal Grammar in Child Second Language Acquisition*

# UNIVERSAL GRAMMAR IN CHILD SECOND LANGUAGE ACQUISITION
## NULL SUBJECTS AND MORPHOLOGICAL UNIFORMITY

USHA LAKSHMANAN
*Southern Illinois University at Carbondale*

JOHN BENJAMINS PUBLISHING COMPANY
AMSTERDAM/PHILADELPHIA

The paper used in this publication meets the minimum requirements of American National Standard for Information Sciences — Permanence of Paper for Printed Library Materials, ANSI Z39.48-1984.

**Library of Congress Cataloging-in-Publication Data**

Lakshmanan, Usha.
Universal grammar in child second language acquisition / Usha Lakshmanan.
    p.    cm. -- (Language acquisition & language disorders : ISSN 0925-0123; v. 10)
    Includes bibliographical references and indexes.
    1. Second language acquisition. 2. Grammar, Comparative and general. I. Title. II. Series.
P118.2. L35     1994
401'.93--dc20                                                           94-26067
ISBN 90 272 2475 7 (Eur.) / 1-55619-247-9 (US) (alk. paper)            CIP

© Copyright 1994 - John Benjamins B.V.
No part of this book may be reproduced in any form, by print, photoprint, microfilm, or any other means, without written permission from the publisher.

John Benjamins Publishing Co. • P.O.Box 75577 • 1070 AN Amsterdam • The Netherlands
John Benjamins North America • 821 Bethlehem Pike • Philadelphia, PA 19118 • USA

# Table of Contents

| | |
|---|---|
| Acknowledgements | viii |
| **1. Syntactic Theory and Child Second Language Acquisition** | 1 |
| 1.0. Introduction | 1 |
| 1.1. The Logical Problem of Language Acquisition | 3 |
| 1.2. UG and Parameterized Grammars | 5 |
| 1.3. The Developmental Problem | 8 |
|    1.3.1. Triggering Data | 9 |
|    1.3.2. Non-Linguistic Maturation Factors | 11 |
|    1.3.3. Linguistic Maturation Factors | 12 |
|    1.3.4. Learning Procedure | 13 |
|    1.3.5. Critical Period for Language Acquisition | 14 |
| 1.4. UG and SLA | 17 |
|    1.4.1. Previous L2 Research | 18 |
|    1.4.2. UG and Child SLA | 19 |
| 1.5. A Note on Methodology | 23 |
| Notes to Chapter 1 | 24 |
| **2. Theoretical Framework** | 27 |
| 2.0. Introduction | 27 |
| 2.1. The Structure of INFL | 29 |
| 2.2. Null Subjects and Rich Agreement | 31 |
| 2.3. The AG/PRO Parameter | 33 |
| 2.4. Null Subjects in Languages without Rich Agreement | 34 |
| 2.5. The Morphological Uniformity Principle | 37 |
| 2.6. Identification of Null Subjects | 41 |
| 2.7. Summary | 45 |
| Notes to Chapter 2 | 45 |

| | |
|---|---|
| **3.  Null Subjects in Developing Grammars** | 47 |
| 3.0.  Introduction | 47 |
| 3.1.  Parameter Setting Accounts of the Null Subject Phenomenon | 49 |
| 3.2.  Morphological Development and Null Subjects in Early Grammars | 51 |
| 3.3.  Predictions of the MUP for SLA | 59 |
| 3.4.  Null Subjects in Developing L2 Grammars | 61 |
| 3.5.  Summary | 66 |
| Notes to Chapter 3 | 67 |
| | |
| **4.  Morphological Uniformity and Null Subjects in Child L2 Grammars** | 71 |
| 4.0.  Introduction | 71 |
| 4.1.  Research Questions | 72 |
| 4.2.  Methods | 73 |
|   4.2.1.  Subjects | 73 |
|   4.2.2.  The Data | 75 |
|   4.2.3.  Data Analysis | 77 |
| 4.3.  Results | 82 |
|   4.3.1  Relations between Null Subjects and Verb Inflections | 82 |
|     4.3.1.1.  Null Subjects | 82 |
|     4.3.1.2.  Null Subjects versus Verb Inflections | 86 |
|     4.3.1.3.  Relations between Inflection Acquisition and Type of Verb Morphology | 90 |
|   4.3.2  Relations between Null Subjects and 'Is-Contexts' | 93 |
|     4.3.2.1.  Developmental Relations between Null Subjects and 'Is Constructions' | 97 |
| 4.4.  Summary | 101 |
| Notes to Chapter 4 | 102 |
| Appendix A | 104 |
| Appendix B | 108 |
| Appendix C | 110 |
| Appendix D | 114 |
| | |
| **5. Discussion and Conclusions** | 118 |
| 5.0.  An Overview | 118 |
| 5.1.  Discussion | 119 |

|  |  |
|---|---|
| 5.1.1. Implications of the Findings for the MUP | 120 |
| 5.1.2. Perpetual Factors and the L1 | 129 |
| 5.1.3. Individual Differences | 138 |
| 5.1.4. Implications for Access to UG and Child SLA | 141 |
| 5.2. Conclusion | 144 |
| Notes to Chapter 5 | 146 |
| References | 148 |
| Index | 159 |

# Acknowledgements

This book is a revised version of my Ph D dissertation (Lakshmanan 1989) that was submitted to the University of Michigan at Ann Arbor. Thanks foremost to the Co-Chairs of my dissertation committee *Susan Gass* and *John Swales* and the two other members of my dissertation committee Marilyn Shatz and Madhav Deshpande for their invaluable advice and tremendous support throughout. I am indebted to Larry Selinker for the many invaluable discussions of the issues addressed in this book. I am grateful to Jürgen Weissenborn and Lydia White for their very helpful comments on the manuscript submitted for review.

The revisions to the manuscript were completed at the Department of Linguistics in Southern Illinois University at Carbondale. I am grateful to Paul Angelis, Chair of the Department of Linguistics and my colleagues in the department for their support and encouragement.

Several other individuals have contributed directly and indirectly to the shaping of this work from its incipient stages to its completion. In particular I thank:

Herlinda Cancino, Kenji Hakuta and John Schumann for making the data from the four child L2 subjects available for the study.

Renu Gupta for undertaking the mammoth task of photocopying numerous transcripts of the child L2 data and making them available to me.

John Warner and Jyothi Sarkar for their help with the analysis and interpretation of the statistical data.

Chang and James Lenze for their help with the graphics.

Sarah Briggs, Sharon Hilles, Nina Hyams, Carolyn Madden, K.P. Mohanan, and India Plough and Bill Rutherford for their very useful discussions.

Patsy Aldridge for her help in tracking down books and articles.

Takae Tsujioka for her tremendous help with the indexing and the formatting of the camera-ready version.

Cornelis Vaes and Lise Winer for their very helpful comments on the formatting of the camera-ready version.

My parents, sisters, brother and Piet Hein for their support and encouragement throughout.

The research reported here was partially funded by a Rackham Block Grant awarded by the Program in Linguistics at the University of Michigan.

# 1 Syntactic Theory and Child Second Language Acquisition

## 1.0. Introduction

Recent advances in linguistic theory within the framework of Government and Binding (Chomsky 1981, 1986a, 1988) have exerted considerable influence on the areas of first language (L1) and second language (L2) acquisition. Within Government and Binding (GB) theory, specific proposals (based on an investigation of adult grammars) have been put forth regarding the properties of Universal Grammar (UG), which are believed to constrain all natural languages. Research within the areas of L1 and L2 acquisition has in turn been concerned with investigating the status of UG in the context of developing grammars. A syntactic property that has received considerable attention within GB theory and the areas of L1 and L2 acquisition is the property of null subjects. Several explanations have been put forth within GB theory to account for the property of null subjects in adult grammars. A very recent explanation of the null subject phenomenon is that of the Morphological Uniformity Principle (MUP), which has been posited by Jaeggli and Safir (1989) as a Universal Principle.

The MUP provides a unified linguistic account of apparently disparate language facts--null subjects and verb inflections. The MUP states that null-subjects are licensed only in languages which which have uniform verb paradigms that is, where all or none of the verb forms in a paradigm are inflected. Examples of such languages are Spanish, Italian, Chinese and Japanese. Languages such as English and French which have non-uniform verb paradigms (that is, where some of the verb forms are inflected and some of the verb forms correspond to the bare stem) do not license null subjects. Certain precise and testable claims for child language development are implied by the

MUP. Assuming that child grammars are "possible grammars", an important prediction of the MUP is that null subjects will occur only in those child grammars which have morphologically uniform verb paradigms but not in those which have morphologically non-uniform verb paradigms.

A fairly stable period has been observed for first language (L1) acquisition of English, during which lexical subjects are optional and are frequently omitted (cf. Brown 1973; Bloom, Lightbown and Hood 1975; Guilfoyle 1984; Hyams 1983, 1986, 1992). During the same period, verb inflections also do not occur. Later, when past and present inflections emerge, null-subjects are abandoned. Jaeggli and Hyams (1988) and Hyams (1992) attempt to explain these facts on the basis of the MUP. They claim that in the early grammars of English (which as a stable linguistic system is a morphologically non-uniform language), the child's initial assumption is that it is [+ uniform]. Hyams and Jaeggli argue that from a learnability-theoretic perspective the [+ uniform] setting is the most restrictive hypothesis. As a result of this initial setting, null subjects are said to occur. Once the child correctly analyzes English as a morphologically non-uniform language, that is, when target-like past and present inflections emerge, the child realizes that subjects of tensed clauses are obligatorily overt and consistently includes them in expected contexts.

This book reports on the findings of a recent study which examined the interlanguage (IL)[1] of four children (two native speakers of Spanish, a native speaker of Japanese, and a native speaker of French) learning English as second language. The purpose of the study was to investigate whether these child second language (L2) learners had access to the MUP. Our central thesis is that there is no strong evidence for child L2 learners' accessibility to the MUP. Specifically, we demonstrate that the predicted relationship between verb inflections and null subjects does not receive major support in child L2 development. Of the four subjects considered in the study, only the IL of one of the Spanish speakers provided (weak) evidence for the MUP whereas the ILs of the other three subjects failed to support its predictions. The findings indicate that child L2 learners of English (regardless of whether their L1 is a null subject language or not) appear to know from the very beginning that overt subjects are obligatory in English. Subject omissions that occur are largely restricted to certain domains and appear to be the result of non-UG factors, specifically perceptual factors interacting with the L1. It is argued that the claims for the status of a universal principle for the MUP are questionable. Instead, our findings tend to support recent proposals (Lillo-Martin 1991; Wang et al 1992) that two different parameterized principles are involved with respect to the null subject phenomenon found in adult grammars.

## 1.1. The Logical Problem of Language Acquisition

The impetus for research within Government and Binding theory (also known as the framework of Principles and Parameters) is the well-known logical problem of language acquisition (Chomsky 1981, 1986a, 1988; Hornstein and Lightfoot 1981; White 1985c), the problem of how human beings come to master the complex properties of the grammar (such as structure dependency, subjacency, binding, etc.) of their native languages in a relatively short period of time and on the basis of input that is not sufficiently rich and precise and in the absence of crucial negative evidence.

The logical problem becomes apparent when one compares the complexities of the language acquired with the "poverty of the stimulus". While the child must necessarily be exposed to input before language acquisition can take place, the input data that are available are deficient in that they do not provide adequate information about complex structures in the language for the child to acquire these on the basis of the input alone. For example, children invariably choose a computationally complex structure dependent rule as in (1a) over a computationally simple structure independent rule as in (1b). (1a) involves movement of the verb in the uppermost clause (i.e. the matrix clause) to the front while (1b) only involves movement of the first verb in a linear ordering of words. Errors such as (1b) have never been attested in the language acquisition literature (both L1 and L2). Children appear to know that sentences such as (1b) are ungrammatical without instruction or negative evidence, or information to the learner that his or her utterance is in some way deviant.

1a. Is the book which is on the table dull
 b. *Is the book which on the table is dull?

To take some other examples: Consider the sentences in (2).

2a. Who did John see?
 b. Who did Fred believe that John saw?
 c. *Who did Fred believe the rumor that John saw?
 d. Fred believed the rumor that John saw Bill.

Sentences such as (2a) suggest to the learner that wh- questions can be formed by moving the Wh direct object to the front of the sentence. Therefore, the learner would be justified in assuming that this rule can be extended to complex sentences such as (2b) which is grammatical and to other complex sentences such as (2c) which is ungrammatical. However, while children produce sentences such as (2b), they fail to produce sentences as in (2c). In other words, they fail to extend the generalization drawn on the basis of sentences such as (2a and 2b) that in English, the wh direct object is moved to the sentence initial position in forming wh questions. Further, this appears to be a problem only for question forms as the statement form in (2d) corresponding to the wh-question form in (2c) is grammatical.

Consider the sentences in (3). Only in (3a) can *them* be coreferential with *the men* (although it can also refer to someone in the discourse context). In (3b), on the other hand, *them* can only refer to someone in the discourse context but not to *the men*.

       3a.    I wonder who the men$_i$ expected to see them$_j$.
       3b.    *The men$_i$ expected to see them$_j$.

Children come to know numerous facts such as (3a) and (3b) without having their attention drawn to them. The question, then, for a theory of grammar is to account for these and other constraints on grammar formation.

It may be argued that children do not make errors such as the use of structure independent rules because they have never heard them before. However, this argument fails to explain why children consistently make certain errors even though they have never encountered them before in the input. An example of such errors is the well-attested tendency on the part of children to extend the past tense regular *-ed* ending to past tense irregular verbs, e.g. *goed, breaked, comed*.

Arguments based on notions of "simplified input" may account for some aspects of the very early stages of acquisition. However, such proposals fail to explain how the child comes to acquire complex linguistic knowledge since by the stage children have to deal with complex linguistic properties, such as sentential embeddings, coreferentiality etc., they will be well beyond the stage of having access to simplified input. The inadequacies of arguments based on notions of simplified input becomes further apparent when we consider that children succeed in determining the properties of grammatically complex sentences plus the ungrammatical sentences. It is difficult to see how children can achieve this if they were to rely on simplified input.

Correction (i.e. negative evidence) of the ungrammatical sentences produced by the child, would perhaps help the child determine which structures are not permitted in the language being learned. However, L1 acquisition research indicates that children do not receive crucial and specific negative evidence regarding the structure of their utterances (Brown and Hanlon 1970).[2,3] One type of negative evidence that children may receive is through the form of incomprehension (similar to that suggested by Schachter (1984) for L2 acquisition). But such indirect evidence is not sufficiently specific to inform learners where exactly they have made an error, whether the failure in communication is the result of incorrect syntax, phonology, morphology or vocabulary. Nor does such indirect evidence indicate what the learner would have to do in order to correct the error (cf. White 1985c ).

While properties of discourse, situational context etc., have an important role to play with respect to certain aspects of language acquisition, they cannot usefully explain the complex properties of language to the learner. For example, they would not be able to explain the grammaticality of sentences such as (3a) versus the ungrammaticality of sentences such as (3b). Yet children appear to have no problems in determining that sentences like the latter are ungrammatical.

While the logical problem of language acquisition was first posed in the context of first language acquisition, it has been argued that the logical problem applies to second language acquisition (SLA) as well (White 1985c; Flynn 1987; Cook 1988; White 1989). L2 learners, like child L1 learners, have to determine the complex properties of the grammar of the target language on the basis of insufficiently rich and precise input. As pointed out by White (1985c:33), the 'inadequacies of simplified input, negative evidence, context and discourse factors seem to be just as true for the L2 acquisition situation as they are for the L1'.[4]

## 1.2. UG and Parameterized Grammars

Recent advances within the framework of Government and Binding theory have offered fresh perspectives on the logical problem of language acquisition. Central to these perspectives is the notion of a parameterized (UG). The notion of UG as a parameterized system is intended to explain how the child arrives at the grammar of a language on the basis of insufficiently rich and precise input *and* to account for the diversity of possible human languages.

Within GB theory, UG is conceived of as a "modular" system which consists of many interacting subsystems. Each subsystem has specific properties (rules and principles) associated with it. The organization of the grammar may be characterized as a T-model as shown in figure 1.1.

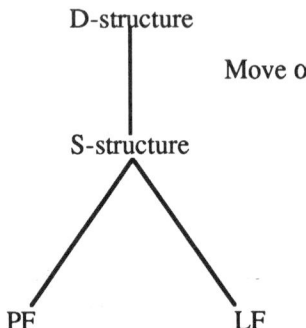

*Fig. 1.1.: T-Model of Universal Grammar*

The T-model shown in Fig. 1.1 determines the universal grammar/core grammar. Sentences are assigned representations at different levels -- D-structure (Deep structure), S-structure, Logical Form (LF) and Phonetic Form (PF). A sentence is grammatical only if it is well-formed at each of these levels. The X-bar theory of phrase structure and the lexicon together comprise D-Structure, which is the 'base component'. S-structure representations are derived from D-structure through the general operation of Move α. D-Structure, S-Structure and Move α make up the 'Syntax'. The S-structure feeds separately into the LF and PF. The mapping from S-structure to PF is called the phonological component which includes processes such as phonological rules, deletion rules etc. The LF component consists of those aspects of meaning that are represented by sentence grammar.

Various subsystems of principles are said to constrain the well-formedness of a representation at the different levels, D-structure, S-structure, LF, and PF. These highly structured and restrictive principles are believed to be specific to the human species and to language. Further, these principles, which are said to hold universally across all languages, are also claimed to be innate, that is, they are believed to characterize the child's pre-linguistic initial state.

Some of the principles of UG are believed to be invariant while others are said to vary along certain parameters; in other words, they are linked to a set of two possible values which represents the limited extent to which language variation is possible with respect to each principle.[5] An example of an invariant UG principle is X-bar theory which constrains the phrase structure component at D-structure (Jackendoff 1977). According to X-bar theory, all phrases must be 'headed' (Stowell 1981). However, languages can vary with respect to the position of the head within its phrase. English, for example, is a 'head first' language where verbs and prepositions precede their complements. Japanese, on the other hand, is a 'head last' language, where verbs and prepositions follow their complements. Another example of a parameterized UG principle is Move $\alpha$ (the principle which states "move any category anywhere"). Languages may vary with respect to what category can be taken as $\alpha$ (NP, PP or VP). A language may permit either one or more of the categories to be moved or it may not permit movement of any of the categories. In addition, languages may vary with respect to the level of application of Move $\alpha$. In English, for example, Wh-movement (an instantiation of Move $\alpha$) is permitted at the level of syntax whereas in Chinese, wh-movement can apply only at the level of logical form (LF) but not in the syntax (C.T.J. Huang 1982).[6] This variation is illustrated by the following examples.

4a. Who$_i$ do you like [e$_i$]
 b. Ni xihuan shei
    'You like who '

The theory of Principles and Parameters assumes an instantaneous model of language acquisition according to which, the child is said to have immediate access to all of the principles of UG and all of the relevant linguistic data. When exposed to data, the child instantly constructs a full fledged adult grammar. Language acquisition within such a theory is viewed as an instantaneous process whereby the child "sets" each of the parameters of UG at a value which is correct for the particular language being learned on the basis of positive evidence.[7] The choice of one value as opposed to another is said to have complex and varying effects on the grammar. Certain features of the input are said to function as "triggers" which facilitate the setting of a particular parameter of UG.

For example, one of the tasks facing a child acquiring English is to discover that in English the head of a phrase precedes its complement. This task is easily achieved since the input data that the child is exposed to will include sentences such as *John ate a cookie* (where the "head" of the VP, i.e. V, precedes its object) but not sentences such as *John a cookie ate*. As Hyams (1986) has stated, word order related parameters will be among the earliest to be set in language development since the relevant information is readily accessible from the environment. Likewise, with respect to Move α, the English speaking child will be exposed to sentences beginning with a wh-word. Such sentences comprise positive evidence to the child that in English Move α applies at the level of syntax. For the Chinese child, on the other hand, such evidence will not be available.[8]

## 1.3. The Developmental Problem

The perspective of UG and Parameterized grammars has exerted considerable influence on L1 acquisition research as is evidenced by the plethora of studies within this framework ( Hyams 1986, 1992; see also the many papers in Lust 1986, 1988; Roeper and Williams 1987; Frazier and de Villiers 1990; Weissenborn, Goodluck and Roeper 1992). It has also had a substantial influence on SLA research (Mazurkeweich 1984; Felix 1985; Clahsen and Muysken 1986; Hilles 1986; Flynn 1987; Bley-vroman 1989; Thomas 1989; White 1985a, 1985b, 1989; see also the many papers in Flynn and O'Neil 1988, Gass and Schachter 1989 and Eubank 1991). The model of language acquistion assumed within the Principles and Parameters framework is an instantaneous model, which does not address the question of how language develops in real time. From a developmental perspective, UG is a prerequisite but not a sufficient condition for real-time acquisition. In addition to UG there are other factors (external and internal) which interact in the process of language acquisition. These factors include input/triggering data, a maturation schedule (non-linguistic and linguistic) and some kind of a evaluation measure/learning procedure for linking the triggering data with the relevant parametric values (see Hilles 1991 for a discussion of these issues).

L1 acquisition researchers, who are also interested in the developmental problem, have been concerned with investigating the extent to which developing grammars are constrained by principles of UG and the interaction between UG and other internal and external factors. In the context of L2 acquisition, it has been claimed that IL grammars are natural languages (Adjemian 1976). We assume that this position is probably correct. Based on this assumption, we would expect that ILs, like other natural languages, are constrained by UG (that is, only a limited set of pre-determined choices/options are available to the L2 learner). As in the case of L1 acquisition, SLA researchers, who are also interested in the developmental problem, have been concerned with investigating the extent to which IL grammars are constrained by UG principles and in the interaction between UG and non-UG related factors.

In what follows, we examine the factors that are believed to interact along with UG in the process of language acquisition. Next, we will examine the notion of a critical period in relation to UG constrained language acquisiton.

*1.3.1. Triggering Data*

The fact that certain principles of grammar are innate neither indicates *when* they will become operative nor *what* exactly is required to activate the principles. Several scholars have adopted the continuity hypothesis in order to address the problem of how a language is acquired in real time (Gleitman and Wanner 1982; Keil 1982; Hyams 1983, 1986, 1992; Pinker 1984). The continuity hypothesis, which is the simplest hypothesis consistent with the instantaneous model of language acquisition, holds that grammatical development is a "continuous process", where the UG principles and parameters remain constant throughout the course of language acquisition. Certain kinds of data (positive evidence) are required to activate the parameter setting process. For example, as we saw earlier, in regard to the UG operation of Move $\alpha$, the English speaking child will initially assume that Move $\alpha$ does not apply in the syntax in English. When the child encounters sentences beginning with a wh-word she will realize that in English, Move $\alpha$ is observed in the syntax. Such triggering data are 'external' to the learner and are clearly not a part of UG.

Various kinds of triggering analyses have been proposed in the literature (Roeper 1978; Pinker 1984; Hyams 1986). Underlying such proposals is the general consensus that if triggering data are absent or do not become available within a biologically specified period, language acquisition will be impossible or at best incomplete (cf. Curtiss 1977). Assuming that the data that trigger parameter setting are always available to the child, it is not clear why certain parameters are not activated sooner than they are. According to White (1982), although input data may be similar at different stages of development, whether certain data will in fact trigger the parameter setting process depends on the child's "intake" which in turn may be dependent on maturation factors (non-linguistic and/or possibly linguistic).

Before we proceed to a discussion of these non-linguistic and linguistic maturation factors, it is relevant to mention some of the problems with respect to triggering data. It is likely that the input that the child is exposed to are "noisy" in that they may include ungrammatical utterances (i.e. contradictory data). This poses a problem for the notion of language acquisition as an instantaneous process of parameter setting since the contradictory data encountered by the child could very well trigger a change in the setting of one or more parameters, which in turn could yield a language which may be quite different in character from the target language. Thus, we will necessarily have to assume that the child's intrinsic constraints are so strong that they effectively nullify the destructive processes of ungrammatical input. It may also be, as has been argued by Roeper and Weissenborn (1990), that contradictory data will never be encountered by the learner in certain domains. If this is the case, then these domains may have a unique triggering function in language acquisition. Learners may have access to knowledge about the unique triggering status of such domains and may therefore be able to ignore contradictory data that they may encounter in other domains.

The problem of "noisy data" becomes particularly apparent when we consider the second language acquisiton context. In addition to grammatical input, L2 learners may be exposed to ungrammatical utterances in the speech of their peers (i.e. other L2 learners). Further, such ungrammatical (including nonstandard) utterances may also characterize the speech of native speakers of the target language, particularly in situations where "accommodation" to the L2 learner is felt to be necessary for the purposes of communication. The problem of ungrammatical data has not been sufficiently addressed in UG based language acquistion research. To take the example of the pro-drop or null subject parameter, it is commonly assumed that since English is a non pro-drop/non null subject language, English speaking children (and L2 learners of English) will never hear pro-drop utterances in English. However, such utterances *are* likely to be encountered in casual speech (for discussion of this issue, see Valian 1990 and Roeper and Weissenborn 1990). A theory of language acquisiton, to be adequate, will need to explain why such casual speech phenomena fail to have serious consequences in the learner's grammars (the issue of contradictory data with respect to the null subject phenomenon is discussed in greater detail in Chapter 3 and Chapter 5).

## 1.3.2. Non-linguistic Maturation Factors

Assuming that triggering data are always present in the input, a question that needs to be addressed is: what causes the child to restructure the grammar at a particular stage? White (1982) attributes the child's restructuring of the grammar to a change in the child's perception of the input which in turn is the outcome of certain factors external to a particular grammar at any stage. These factors include increasing memory, attention span, and general maturation factors. According to White, UG principles may be viewed as interacting with the child's perception of the data at any particular stage of language development. When the child's attention is switched to certain aspects of the data, the child's grammar also changes. Thus, it is only when we take into account the child's changing perception of the data that we can reasonably state that the principles of UG are activated by the triggering data. Certain data may require an analysis that exceeds the child's capabilities at certain stages and therefore may not be relevant to the child. For instance, certain data may be manifest only in complex sentences. Because of limitations in memory and attention span, young children will be unable to process complex sentences. Therefore, such data would not be relevant until their ability to attend to and remember more of the data increases. White (1982) illustrates this point with the example of the structure dependency principle. At the beginning stages children may produce utterances such as (5):

5. Is the man tall?

However, at this same stage, they will be unable to ask the more complex question as in (6).

6. Is the man who is tall in the room?

Even if utterances such as (6) occur in the input during the early stages, such data may not be perceived by children as relevant in order for the structure dependency operation to be activated. Data such as (6) will become relevant only at the stage when children are able to process complex utterances.

As stated earlier, adult L2 learners and most child L2 learners will have undergone the relevant non-linguistic maturational development prior to learning a second language. Hence, it may be argued that non-linguistic factors such as memory, attention span etc., may not operate in the same way in L2 acquisition as in L1 acquisition. However, this must not be taken to mean that the L2 learners' perception of the data does not change. L2 learners, unlike the L1 learner, have a prior instantiation of UG, namely the L1. In terms of their prior experience, they may be said to know the exact effects of setting a particular parameter a certain way. Knowledge of each of these effects involves, as a necessary concomitant, an extensive knowledge of the facts specific to L1 (i.e. the peripheral aspects, such as the lexicon, etc.). Thus, as Flynn and Manuel (1991:140) have stated, in comparison with the L1 learner, the L2 learner will have to change 'not only a hypothesis concerning a parameter value but a whole range of interrelated language-specific facts '. This task will necessarily involve the re-interpretation of each of the effects of parameter setting in the L2 in relation to the language specific facts of L2. Knowledge of the effects of parameter setting in the L1 along with the interrelated language specific facts of L1 may influence the L2 learners' perception of the L2 data which in turn may influence the learners' progress in the task of restructuring the grammar. The above explanation, points to an important difference between child L2 acquisition and the adult L2 acquisition. The child L2 learner will have less confirmed notions about the effects of setting a particular parameter in the L1 and also less extensive knowledge about the language specific facts of the L1 compared to the adult learner. Thus, the child L2 learner may face fewer problems in the task of restructuring the grammar in the L2 (a detailed discussion of the role of perceptual factors in L2 acquisition is presented in Chapter 5).

*1.3.3. Linguistic Maturation Factors*

According to Borer and Wexler (1987) principles of UG, like any other instance of biological maturation, may also take time to develop. Since many aspects of the brain are known to mature after birth, to the extent that linguistic properties are situated in the brain, then linguistic properties themselves may be expected to mature.

One candidate for a maturational universal is the principle of A-binding.[9] Borer and Wexler (1987) propose that at the earliest stages of development the child's grammar lacks the principle of A-binding. This principle is believed to mature at a later point. As a consequence, the child is unable to produce or interpret verbal passives (or raising constructions) at the early stages. Borer and Wexler also invoke the notion of a linguistic maturation schedule to account for other aspects of child language, such as the overgeneralization of the causative construction to non-causative verbs, e.g. *John giggled me* (= John made me giggle).[10]

While it may be difficult to distinguish between cases where the data trigger the relevant UG principle or where a principle is maturationally activated, it is possible that both a non-linguistic maturation schedule and a linguistic maturation schedule are involved in the process of language acquisition, for bringing about the conditions conducive for parameter setting. While these are internal to the organism, they are external to the child's grammar at any stage, and therefore not a part of UG.

*1.3.4. Learning Procedure*

As discussed earlier, only positive evidence is typically available to the child learner. The child does not receive direct negative evidence about ungrammatical sentences. This being the case, the question that may be posed is, how are the values of the parameters learned from experience? The learnability problem is that if the child overgeneralizes, that is, selects a grammar that produces too large a language, then no amount of positive evidence can cause the child to arrive at the correct grammar since all of the new positive data will be generated by the overgeneralized grammar. Specifically, this problem applies to those cases where the overgeneralized grammar is a superset of the correct language. On the other hand, if the child undergeneralizes, that is chooses the smaller grammar (which is the subset of the correct language), then positive evidence will indicate to the child that the grammar selected is not the correct one.

A principle that has been recently proposed in the language acquisition literature to account for the learnability problem (Berwick 1985; Manzini and Wexler 1987) is the subset principle. The subset principle states that given two values of a parameter, the child will select the value which yields the smaller language. The learning procedure implied by the subset principle is consistent with that implied by markedness hierarchies since the smaller language is in essence the least marked or most accessible grammar. Some kind of learning procedure similar to that specified by the subset principle may be required in order to map triggering data onto parametric values. Suppose, for example, that a certain parameter has a set of two values (x) and (y) associated with it. Selection of the value (x) would generate a language L(x) and selection of the value (y) would generate a language L(y). Let us further assume that L(x) is a subset of L(y). Since L(x) is a smaller language than L(y), it is also the simplest and most accessible of the two grammars. In this situation, the subset principle predicts that the learner's first choice will be the value which generates L(x). If L(x) is the correct language, the learner will never encounter any evidence that suggests otherwise and will therefore remain with the chosen value. If the value L(x) selected is incorrect, that is, if L(y) is the correct language, then there will be positive evidence that an incorrect selection has been made. When such evidence is encountered, the learner will switch to the parameter value which produces language L(y).

The basic rationale of the subset principle does appear to be useful in explaining at least certain aspects of first language acquisition. Its relevance for the second language acquisition situation is, however, not fully known. Zobl (1988) stated that the subset principle, in its current formulation may be inapplicable to second language acquisition--at least in the early stages (for similar discussion see White 1989). This is because, as Zobl has demonstrated, L2 learners may initially adopt a wider grammar (i.e. the grammar of their L1) before proceeding to a narrower grammar (i.e. the grammar of the L2), which is contrary to the predictions of the subset principle. Thus, Zobl suggests that the subset principle will necessarily have to be modified in order to enhance its relevance in the L2 context.[11]

Learning procedures specified by the subset principle or versions of the subset principle may be internal to the learner, and may be the outcome of the interaction of non-linguistic / linguistic maturation factors with principles of UG. However, like triggering data, and the linguistic and non-linguistic maturational schedule, such procedures cannot be considered a part of UG.

*1.3.5. Critical Period for Language Acquisition*

There are several versions of the critical period hypothesis, of which the best known and the strongest formulation is the original statement by Lenneberg (1967). Lenneberg argued for a biologically determined critical period for language acquisition. According to Lenneberg, the beginning stage of the critical period is restricted by lack of maturation. Its termination is associated with functional changes in the brain such as the loss of brain plasticity and specialization of brain functions to one hemisphere. The strong formulation of the critical period hypothesis predicts (incorrectly) that no first language acquisition is possible if the child is not exposed to language before puberty. The weak version of the hypothesis states that while some language learning is possible after puberty, native-like abilities will be unachievable and the process of language development will become more irregular and fall further short of native levels of achievement (the later the age of onset).

While Lenneberg's specific claims in regard to the relation between the functional changes in the brain and the critical period are questionable, his overall proposal for the existence of a critical period does seem to be reasonable. Gleitman (1986) examined studies of children acquiring a first language in normal setttings and concluded that the course of language acquisition is characterized by certain "milestones" through which children proceed at roughly the same stage of language development. These milestones have been observed irrespective of environmental variation such as cultural or social class differences in child rearing patterns or in caretaker speech. The lack of effect of environmental variation along with the presence of milestones suggest that maturational constraints operate on first language learning.

The best known test case of Lenneberg's original formulation of the critical period hypothesis is that of Genie (Curtiss 1977). Genie spent the early years of her life deprived of social and linguistic contact until her discovery at the age of 13.7. In terms of Lenneberg's claims, she was well beyond the end point of the critical period. Despite this, Genie did acquire some language. However, her language development was irregular when compared with normal learning sequences, and even until the final stages when she was observed, she had failed to achieve native-like proficiency, particularly in morphology and syntax. Her ability in regard to vocabulary and semantics surpassed her ability in syntax, morphology, and phonology, and likewise, her comprehension far exceeded her production. The evidence from Genie's language development is consistent with the weak version of the hypothesis that language learning is possible after puberty, but that it will be irregular and incomplete after this point.

Long (1990) examined studies on the maturational constraints in language development, and concluded that language specific maturational constraints are operative in both child first language acquisition and child second language acquisition and further, that there are critical/sensitive periods during which language learning is successful, after which it is "irregular and incomplete". Maturational constraints would therefore explain why adults, but not children, generally fail to achieve native-like ability in a second language. Long discusses the findings of long term studies on child and adult second language acquisition which indicate that it is impossible to achieve native-like competence in phonology after the age of six; likewise, the acquisition of morphology, syntax and semantics appear to be difficult starting later than the early teens.

In a recent study, Johnson and Newport (1989) tested native Korean and Chinese speakers who had arrived in the United States between the ages of 3 and

39 years, and who had resided in the United States between 3 and 26 years at the time their study was conducted. The subjects were tested on a wide variety of structures of English grammar through the use of a grammaticality judgement task. The study found that those subjects who had arrived earlier (i.e. before the age of seven) performed significantly better than those who had arrived later, leading the authors to conclude that young children are more successful second language learners than older children and adults.

Flynn and Manuel (1991) present new evidence from several L1 and L2 studies which considerably weakens the claims that there is a critical period for language learning and that adult L2 acquisition is qualitatively different from child language acquisition. According to Flynn and Manuel, a serious limitation of earlier studies that have argued for differences between the child L1 learner and the adult L2 learner in regard to ultimate level of attainment is that these studies focus on language specific surface phenomena which are related to the "periphery" of language knowledge, as opposed to the more abstract subsystems of principles and rules of UG. Flynn and Manuel further state that general inductive learning mechanisms may be involved in the acquisition of the peripheral aspects of language and that it is precisely with respect to these peripheral aspects that adults may be expected to be less successful than children. On the other hand, with respect to the acquisition of the "core" aspects of the language, adult L2 learners from diverse L1 backgrounds, 'achieve mental states for the L2 that involve a deductive component for the language that goes beyond any available data and beyond any explicit teaching'. Flynn and Manuel present experimental evidence to show that adults use abstract principles of UG even in those situations where inductive learning mechanisms could have been resorted to.

Overall, the evidence seems to suggest that some aspects of language learning are influenced by a critical/sensitive period. However, more empirical evidence is needed to resolve questions concerning the exact nature and length of the critical period and the specific aspects of language learning that are affected by it. In the context of our present framework, we may consider the relation, if any, between the critical period for language acquisition and access to UG. Several possibilities are immediately apparent. One possibility is that UG is available only during the critical period but not beyond this stage. A second possibility is that the critical period is the period during which parameters mature or certain conditions (i.e. conditions resulting from the interaction of triggering data with non-linguistic maturation factors) become conducive for parameter setting. A third possibility is that the learning procedure which maps the triggering data onto parametric values is operative only during the critical period. A final possibility is that UG and all of the other factors (external and internal) are most easily available during the critical period and become less and less accessible beyond this point. (for similar discussion see Hilles 1989).

As we discussed earlier, UG alone is not adequate for successful language acquisition. Several other factors are required to make language acquisition possible. Unsuccessful or incomplete language acquisition could result from the following possibilities: (i) UG is not available; (ii) the triggering data are not present in the input to the learner; (iii) the linguistic and non-linguistic maturation schedules are not functioning normally; or (v) the learning procedure which links the triggering data with the parameter values is inactive or unavailable. In our present study, we will consider UG, by definition, as distinct from those internal and external factors that are believed to interact in the process of language acquisition. By access to UG we mean accessibility to only the principles of UG and it is only in this sense that we will address the notion of access to UG. At the same time, however, when and where evidence from our data is suggestive or requires it, we will attempt to throw light on the role of non-UG factors in SLA.

## 1.4. UG and SLA

The notion of UG and parameterized grammars is relevant in explaining the logical problem of L2 acquisition. L2 syntactic development, like L1 acquisition, may be viewed as a process whereby the learner sets the appropriate values of the UG parameters relevant for the target language on the basis of positive evidence. However, the task of the L2 learner is confounded by the fact that in the L2 context, there is input from at least two languages which may differ with respect to the instantiation of a particular UG Principle or Parameter. Thus, while it is possible that the L1 and L2 share the same settings with respect to a particular parameter, as White (1985b, 1989) and others have suggested, the following possibilities may also obtain in an L2 situation. (i) The L1 may have a certain parameter set differently from that in the L2. (ii) A parameter which is operative in the L1 is not present in the L2. (iii) A parameter that is at work in L2 is absent in the L1.

It would be relevant, therefore, to investigate whether the selection of one value, as opposed to another, along a certain parameter has complex and varying effects throughout the development of the IL grammar, and whether certain aspects of the input data act as "triggers" which facilitate the process of setting the correct value along a certain parameter in the L2. The notion of UG and parameterized grammars will enable us to make precise claims regarding the nature and development of IL; ideas which can, moreover, be tested. Further, an examination of IL grammars within the framework of a parameterized system of UG will enable us to incorporate within a common theory conflicting accounts of the SLA process: those offered by the Contrastive analysis hypothesis which holds that the L1 guides L2 acquisition and those offered by the Creative Construction hypothesis which holds that L2 acquisition is guided by universal developmental processes (see Flynn 1987 for a detailed discussion of these ideas).

*1.4.1. Previous L2 Research*

A question that has been the focus of much controversy in recent Second language acquisition research within the framework of Principles and parameters is whether IL grammars are constrained by principles of UG. Several claims have been made on the basis of experimental evidence in regard to the issue of the availability of UG in adult second language acquisition. The focus of much of this UG-based L2 research (in the 1980s) has largely been on the adult L2 learner, and the point of comparison in nearly all cases has been with the monolingual child L1 learner (for a similar view see Felix 1991). Currently, there are three different hypotheses regarding the availability of UG in adult L2 acquisition: 'Direct Access to UG', 'indirect access to UG' and 'No access to UG' (for a discussion of these three positions see Cook 1988 and White 1989). According to the Direct Access to UG position, adult L2 grammars are constrained by UG principles in the same way as child L1 grammars are (Mazurkewich 1984). The indirect access to UG position, on the other hand, proposes that UG principles are available to adult L2 learners through the mediation of the L1 (White 1985a; Schwartz 1987). Where a parameterized principle is involved, the L1 setting is initially transferred and if this setting is different from the setting in the L2, parameter resetting takes place in ways that are constrained by UG. The 'No access to UG' hypothesis, on the other hand, holds that UG principles are no longer available to adult L2 learners and that adult L2 acquisition proceeds through the use of general problem solving procedures (Clahsen and Muysken 1986; Schachter 1990).

## 1.4.2. UG and Child SLA

In contrast to the adult L2 learner, the child L2 learner has largely been ignored in UG based SLA research. This trend in recent L2 research is very different from the situation that existed in the 1970s, when child second language acquisition was being actively researched (Huang 1970; Cancino, Rosansky and Schumann 1974; Dulay and Burt 1974; Hakuta 1974, 1976; Milon 1974; Cazden, Cancino, Rosansky and Schumann 1975; Selinker, Swain and Dumas 1975; Wong-Fillmore 1976; Adams 1978; Ravem 1978; Wode 1978; Felix 1980 and many others). These early child L2 studies addressed several issues including issues such as: the role of developmental universals versus the L1, the similarities and differences between child L1 and child L2, and child L2 and adult L2, L2 developmental stages (particularly with respect to negation and interrogatives), individual differences, and the role of pre-fabricated utterances and so on. Much of this research, however, tended to be largely descriptive in nature and research at the explanatory level was by and large lacking.[12] Although there was a concern with developmental universals in this early SLA research, the interpretation of the term universals tended to be rather general and not sufficiently precise (for a discussion of this issue see Lightbown and White 1988). However, this state of affairs is not surprising since the connections with developments in linguistic theory, unlike in the 1980s, were not particularly strong during the 1970s.

Although much of the UG based SLA research in the 1980s has been primarily concerned with the adult L2 learner, this trend is currently in the process of undergoing a change as once again SLA researchers are becoming interested in investigating child L2 acquisition. Thus far, advances in UG based SLA research have mainly been unidirectional: developments within linguistic theory have influenced SLA research but similar influences in the reverse direction have not been equally apparent. Child L2 grammars, in this regard, can be valuable in helping to change this trend. It is a generally accepted view that child L2 learners, unlike adult L2 learners, are typically successful with respect to ultimate attainment of the target L2 (Krashen, Long and Scarcella 1979; Felix 1985; Johnson and Newport 1989; Larsen-Freeman and Long 1991). In many of the adult L2 studies, the tendency has been to assume that specific proposals for a UG principle are indeed correct, which assumption has lead to certain predictable consequences. If a proposed principle is not observed as being operative in adult L2 grammars, the conclusion that is typically drawn is one which is consistent with the position that adult L2 acquisition is not constrained by UG. An alternative view, namely that the linguists' proposals for a specific UG principle may be incorrect is rarely entertained (for similar discussion see Gass 1993). In view of the success that child L2 learners achieve in acquiring the L2, child L2 grammars may be more valuable in testing the correctness of specific theoretical proposals.

Child L2 grammars may be even more valuable in this regard than child L1 grammars. In child L1 acquisition, the development of language is usually in step with the development of non-linguistic maturation factors such as memory, perception etc., whereas in child SLA it is generally not the case (Gass and Ard 1980). Since unlike child L1 learners, most child L2 learners are cognitively more mature, this fact should enable us to more effectively choose between linguistic based explanations versus cognitive-processing based accounts of developing grammars.

Detailed comparisons of child L2 grammars with child L1 and adult L2 grammars should also enable us to better understand the role of biological factors in accessing UG in the L2 (Felix 1991). As stated earlier, in order to effectively address the developmental problem of child first language acquisition, some scholars have adopted the continuity hypothesis, which holds that principles of UG are available throughout the stages of language acquisition from the initial state (S0), through the intermediate states (S1, S2, S3...) to ST (adult grammar-steady state). The relevant principles/settings are activated through an interaction with the input data. In contrast, proponents of the 'maturation hypothesis' have argued that certain aspects of UG may be maturationally driven rather than being driven by aspects of the input data (that is, different principles of UG will emerge at different times).

Most child L2 learners, like adult learners will have undergone the relevant maturational development prior to learning a second language. If the L2 learner proceeds through the same sequence in regard to a certain parameter as the L1 learner, then this would be an indication that UG principles/parameters may not be maturationally driven. Moreover, by comparing L1 and L2 developmental sequences, we may be able to separate maturational aspects of UG from other aspects that are triggered by data.

As we saw earlier, the logical problem of language acquisition applies to the SLA context, in particular that of child SLA. Child L2 learners, like the child L1 learner, acquire the complex properties of the grammar of the target language on the basis of input that is not sufficiently rich and precise. The success on the part of children in acquiring a second language, when compared to the incomplete learning on the part of the adult L2 learners has been generally taken to mean that Child L2 = Child L1. However, this view ignores the fact that the child L2 learner has previous knowledge of another language -- the L1. In other words, the child L2 learner approaches the task of learning an L2 with a prior instantiation of many or all of the UG principles.

The question then is, do child L2 learners have access to UG principles and parameters in acquiring the L2? There are three logically possible answers to this question of child second language learnability, all of which are determined by how we define the second language learners' "initial state" (Rutherford 1986).

The first logical possibility is that child L2 learners have "direct access" to UG principles and parameters; in other words, the L2 is acquired in the same way as the L1 is acquired. Children acquiring an L2 will have access to all of the principles and parameters of UG in its initial state. In learning the L2, they will begin with the parameters "set" at the default values and determine the values of these parameters that are appropriate for the L2, in exactly the same way as is done by the L1 learner; in other words, constrained by UG. As Sharwood Smith (1988) has stated, this process is a "recreative" one since the L2 learner "recreates" the L2 grammar as was done for the L1. In this view, regardless of whether the L1 settings differ from or match the L2 settings, the L1 is ignored and plays no part in the developing IL grammar. If child L2 learners have "direct access" to UG we would expect child L1 and L2 developmental sequences to be identical.

The second logical possibility is that the child L2 learner has "indirect access" to UG. In this view, child SLA is constrained by UG as in the "direct access" situation . However, there is one major difference. Many or all of the principles of UG may no longer be "open" but may be "set" in L1 terms. If the L1 setting differs from the L2 setting, then "resetting" will need to be carried out. As Sharwood-Smith (1988) has stated, this process of indirect access to UG is essentially a "reconstructive" one involving three phases. During the first phase, the L1 instantiations are applied to the L2 on the basis of the perceived input. The second phase involves the "recreative" application of UG (on the basis of positive evidence) in those areas where the L1 is not relevant, that is, those cases where either a parameter has not yet been set in the L1 or a parameter is not operative in the L1. During the third phase, which is essentially one of "reorganization", the results of the first phase (mapping of L1 settings to the L2) are revised on the basis of positive evidence. This reorganization is carried out within the absolute constraints of UG.

The third possibility is that there is no access to UG. In the "no access" situation, the L1 functions as an initial "template" and the L1 settings are transferred directly to the developing L2 grammar (Sharwood-Smith refers to this possibility as 'Parasitic development '). UG is no longer operative although it may appear to be active in those cases where the L1 and L2 share the same settings. Where the L1 setting differs from the L2 setting, "resetting" cannot occur since UG is no longer available. In the absence of UG, the L2 learner will have to build the IL grammar by resorting to some general learning principles so that the IL output gradually approximates to the target language. The interlanguage resulting from this process may resemble (at least initially) the interlanguage resulting from the process of "indirect access". However, it will also differ from the "indirect access" situation in two ways. First, since UG is no longer available, the IL may be expected to contain some 'non-natural' features that could never appear in any L1. Second, the clustering of linguistic properties that must result from an actual parameter setting may not be manifested in the IL .

The three possibilities of "direct access", "indirect access", and "no access" in child SLA are valid only on the assumption that a posited principle or parameter is indeed a part of UG. This conclusion is relevant in the context of our framework, since it implies that UG is accessible to the child L2 learner as well as the child L1 learner. In other words, we would expect either the "direct access" or the "indirect access" situation to apply in the context of child SLA. However, there is another alternative. It may be that the claims for a universal status of a specific principle of UG are not supported in child SLA. In this event we would expect evidence for the "no access" explanation to be manifested in the IL of the child L2 learners. To take the case of the MUP, if it is found that null-subjects and inflections are not related in the IL grammars of child L2 learners, then there could be at least one of two reasons involved. One reason would be that child L2 learners, unlike child L1 learners, do not have access to the MUP. An alternative explanation would be that the MUP, at least in its current formulation, is perhaps not a principle of UG. In view of children's success in learning a second language, one may be compelled to choose the latter explanation (this, of course, requires the assumption that L2 data provide a forum for evaluating linguistic theory). However, as in much of UG based SLA research, clear cut evidence may not be forthcoming. It may be that the predictions of the MUP are supported in the case of a few child L2 learners but not in the case of other child L2 learners. On the basis of such findings, one would have to necessarily conclude that some child L2 learners have access to UG while others do not. Such a scenario would serve to illustrate the difficulties involved in resolving the question of L2 access to UG. Thus, a challenge currently facing SLA research is to adequately explain not only the commonalties underlying the language acquisition process but also the variation (including the extent of such variation) that is possible.

## 1.5. A Note on Methodology

In our study, we confine ourselves to longitudinal production data of children who were acquiring English as L2 in a naturalistic setting. The analysis that we present is based on the transcripts of longitudinal data that were gathered previously by other SLA researchers. The data on the two native speakers of Spanish were reported in Cazden, Cancino, Rosansky and Schumann (1975); the data on the native speaker of French were reported in Gerbault (1978), and the data on Uguisu were obtained from Hakuta (1975) (a detailed discussion of the data is presented in chapter 4). Our decision to use production data (rather than introspective evidence), and to carry out a reanalysis (as opposed to collecting original data) needs some explanation.

A method traditionally adopted in studying adult linguistic competence is "grammaticality judgments". This is considered to be an effective method for inquiring into the linguistic competence of a speaker. This method is intended to remove deficient data (that is, data which are affected by performance factors such as memory or attention). Also, through this method, certain types of abstract knowledge, which are evidenced rarely in production, can be obtained.

UG based studies on adult SLA have typically used gramaticality judgement tasks to tap linguistic knowledge of the L2. However, this type of introspective evidence may not be readily available to child learners. Moreover, it is felt that the relationship between the development of verb inflections and disappearance of null-subjects, which is the focus of this study, can be best addressed by longitudinal production data, rather than through introspective evidence. We assume, along with Hyams (1986) that consistent use of a particular structure, regardless of whether or not it matches the target criterion, is indicative of certain rules and processes. Thus, by confining our data base to certain systematic and productive processes, it is hoped that some of the problems associated with the use of production data for grammatical analysis will have been avoided.

Rather than collecting our own data, we chose to analyze data reported in previous studies. As new theories are proposed, it is important to evaluate these in the light of the same data. As Felix (1991) has pointed out, the problem if any, in current SLA research is not lack of data. Rather, the problem lies with the conclusions that have been drawn on the basis of data that is currently available. As Felix (1991:92) observes, recent developments in linguistic theory have 'taught us that fundamental issues are frequently not resolved by more and new data, but rather by carefully examining the rationale and conceptual perspective underlying opposing views'. As several scholars undertake an indepth examination of the same data, they are likely to arrive at different and more reasonable interpretations of the data, all of which can only serve to deepen our understanding of the SLA process.

## Notes to Chapter 1

1. The term 'Interlanguage' was first popularized in a seminal paper by Selinker (1972) to distinguish between the qualitative differences in the strategies of first and second language learning. In its most general sense the term refers to the systematic linguistic behavior of L2 learners. In this study, we use the term 'Interlanguage' to refer to developing L2 grammars; thus, while the term is useful in distinguishing developing L2 grammars from child L1 grammars, it also leaves open the possibility that child L1 grammars and interlanguage grammars share some essential commonalties.

2. Recently, it has been suggested that negative evidence is available to the L1 learner (Hirsh-Pasek et al 1984; Bohannon and Stanowicz 1988). However, as White (1989) has stated, the error types cited in these studies as triggering negative evidence do not include the complex properties of language which a theory of UG seeks to explain.

3. For more recent arguments in support of the position that children do not receive specific and crucial negative evidence see Morgan and Travis (1989).

4. L2 learners, in a formal learning situation, do receive negative evidence in the form of overt corrections. However, as White (1985c) stated, such negative evidence may not account for all the complex properties of L2 syntax acquisition, specially if the L2 learners fail to make the relevant errors. White (ibid) suggested that there may be some specific cases where negative evidence may be useful. More recently, White (1992) investigated the effects of overt instruction concerning adverb placement in English. She found that the group that had specifically been instructed in adverb placement came to know that short verb movement (i.e. past the adverb) is prohibited in

English. White (1990/1991) also compared the short term effects and long term effects of overt instruction and concluded that negative evidence has short term effects but not long term ones.

5.  It is not fully clear whether the set of possible parametric values is always limited to the values of [+] and [-]. In the context of language acquisition, for example, it is possible to conceive of a parameter as being initially set at a neutral value, as opposed to the [+] or [ - ] setting.

6.  Huang (1984) has stated that at LF, the interpretation of wh questions in Chinese and English are identical even though there is no wh movement at the level of syntax.

7.  As Chomsky (1988) has stated, setting of parameters is only part of the process involved in language acquisition and does not account for how the peripheral aspects of language such as vocabulary items are acquired.

8.  A child learning Chinese would not have any direct evidence about the nature of the representations at the level of Logical Form. As Hyams (1986) has stated, this implies that LF representations are by and large a priori.

9.  More recently, specific proposals have been put forth for a maturational schedule with respect to non-thematic (i.e. syntactic) systems. According to one position ( Lebeaux 1988; Radford 1990; Guilfoyle and Noonan 1992) child L1 acquirers of English are believed to go through an initial lexical/thematic stage where functional categories and related mechanisms such as such as the Case system, Inflectional system, Complementizer system and the Determiner system are absent. Radford (1990) specifically claimed that functional categories and non-thematic systems become operative roughly around the age of 24 months. This position is far from being uncontroversial, however, and many L1 researchers have argued that functional categories and related mechanisms are available from the very beginning (e.g. Deprez and Pierce 1993; Poeppel and Wexler 1993; Valian 1992)

10. However, see Weinberg (1987) for an alternative account of the same language acquisition facts which is consistent with the continuity hypothesis.

11. For a critique of Zobl's arguments see Van Buren (1988).

12. The morpheme acquisition studies (Dulay and Burt 1973, 1974) are a good example of this trend in L2 research. The findings of these studies indicated that there is a largely invariant order in which morphemes are acquired by child L2 learners of English regardless of the L1 background. Explanations that have been offered for the order of acquisition of morphemes have primarily been based on external criteria such as frequency in the input (see Larsen-Freeman 1976) and semantic complexity (see

Hakuta 1974). However, these external factors do not in of themselves sufficiently account for the development of morphemes. What is needed is a more principled explanation that is based on factors internal to the learner as opposed to external ones.

# 2 Theoretical Framework

## 2.0. Introduction

The null subject parameter, or what is commonly referred to as the "pro-drop" parameter has received considerable attention within GB theory (Chomsky 1981, 1982; Rizzi 1982; Jaeggli 1980, 1982; Safir 1982, Jaeggli and Safir 1989). The pro-drop parameter is intended to determine "...whether the subject of a clause can be suppressed" (Chomsky 1988:64). Languages are said to vary with respect to whether they instantiate the [+ pro-drop] value or the [- pro-drop] value. In [+ pro-drop] languages such as Italian and Spanish, the subject of a tensed clause can be dropped. In non-pro-drop languages such as English and French, the lexical realization of the subject is obligatory.[1,2] Several proposals have been offered to account for the null subject or pro-drop phenomenon. While these proposals differ in certain respects, there is a general consensus that the pro-drop phenomenon is related to the properties of the INFL(ection) node. Taraldsen (1978) observed that several pro-drop languages have fairly rich systems of agreement. It has therefore been generally assumed that the possibility of dropping a subject from a tensed clause is directly dependent on whether the identity of the null subject can be recovered from the verb agreement endings. Hence, in most accounts (Chomsky 1981, 1982, 1986a, 1988; Jaeggli 1980, 1982; Rizzi 1982; Safir 1982; Hyams 1983, 1986 among others) the term pro-drop has been restricted to richly inflected languages such as Italian and Spanish. However, it has been observed by Mohanan (1983) and C.T.J. Huang (1984) that the correlation between richness of inflection and pro-drop is at best a tendency and not an absolute principle. There are languages that do not have agreement and yet allow the suppression of subjects. Japanese, Chinese, Korean and Malayalam are examples of such languages. In addition, there are languages such as German and Icelandic which are richly inflected and yet do not allow null referential subjects. Only null expletives are permitted in these languages.

Recently, Jaeggli and Safir (1989) proposed an analysis of the null subject phenomenon which is intended to solve the problems inherent in previous analyses. Their account of the pro-drop phenomenon departs in important ways from earlier explanations. Crucial to their account is the notion of morphological uniformity which they claim is a UG principle. Languages may be said to vary with respect to whether they have morphologically uniform verb paradigms (i.e. where all the verb forms are inflected or none of them are inflected) or morphologically non-uniform verb paradigms (i.e. where some verb forms are inflected and some are uninflected). According to Jaeggli and Safir, only languages that are morphologically uniform license null subjects whereas languages which are not morphologically uniform do not allow null subjects. In their view, the occurrence or non-occurrence of null-subjects is considered as simply an effect of whether a language instantiates the [+uniform] or [-uniform] value. As we will see in Chapter 3, the theoretical construct of the MUP, on which the present study is based, has certain important implications for L1 and L2 acquisition.

This chapter is organized as follows. In section 2.1, we discuss aspects of GB theory which are relevant to our analyses of the SLA data. Specifically, we will examine the internal structure of INFL, which plays a crucial role in many accounts of the null subject phenomenon. In section 2.2 we briefly discuss previous analyses of the null-subject phenomenon in richly inflected languages. Specifically, we discuss the original formulation of the pro-drop parameter presented in Rizzi (1982) which forms the basis of most accounts of the null subject phenomenon. In section 2.3, we examine a version of the pro-drop parameter, namely, the AG/PRO parameter proposed by Hyams (1983, 1986). In section 2.4, we present C.T.J. Huang's (1984) analysis which is intended to show that pro-drop also occurs in languages lacking agreement. In section 2.5 we discuss in detail the theoretical construct of the Morphological Uniformity Principle (MUP) proposed by Jaeggli and Safir (1989). In so doing, we discuss the notion of morphological uniformity and its relation to the null-subject phenomenon. In the final section, we discuss the "Identification requirement " which along with the MUP is intended to provide an adequate account of the properties of adult null subject and non null subject languages.

## 2.1. The Structure of INFL

According to X-bar theory of phrase structure syntax, which is believed to be a universal principle, phrases are hierarchically structured projections of their heads as is illustrated in (1). The different phrasal categories or maximal projections such as NP (N"), VP (V"), PP (P"), AP (A") etc. are said to be uniformly structured. There is a terminal head X (where X may be N, V, P, and A etc.) which must match its phrasal projection ( i.e. an NP must be headed by an N, a VP must be headed by a V and so on). The phrase can contain complements of the head which will be sisters to the head. The head of the phrase along with its complement forms the X' level. The phrase can also contain an adjunct, which will be a sister to X'. X' is recursive and so an X' and its adjunct together form another X'. Specifiers occur outside the X' level. X' and the Specifier together form the maximal projection or the highest level XP (=X").

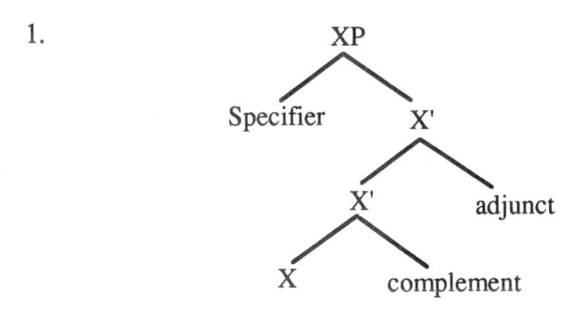

1.
```
              XP
            /    \
      Specifier   X'
                /    \
              X'      adjunct
            /    \
           X      complement
```

In earlier work (Chomsky 1981), the functional categories of INFL(ection) (which consists of the tense and agreement features) and C(omplementizer) were not represented as participating in the X-bar theory of phrase structure syntax. In more recent formulations (for example, the Barriers system proposed by Chomsky 1986b), the X-bar theory of phrase is extended to the functional categories of INFL and C, and these elements, like the lexical categories of N, V, A, P are said to head their own phrasal projections of IP and CP respectively as shown in (2). Like other phrasal projections, IP and CP contain a SPEC position and a complement position (INFL takes VP as its complement and C takes IP as its complement). Whereas in Chomsky (1981), the subject position is represented as the NP immediately dominated by S (=IP in the Barriers system), the subject position is represented as the SPEC of IP.

2.
```
         CP
        /  \
      Spec  C'
           /  \
          C    IP
              /  \
           Spec   I'
                 /  \
                I    VP
```

According to the Extended Projection Principle (Chomsky 1981), which is considered to be a universal, all sentences (i.e. IPs) must have a subject position. INFL, which is the head of IP, consists of a bundle of (abstract) features, specifically that of Tense and AGR(eement). Languages can vary with respect to whether the INFL features of Tense and AGR(eement) are overtly realized on the verb.

AGR includes a bundle of features for person, number, and gender that are linked to the subject. AGR can be either positively or negatively specified (+/- AGR). Tense, like AGR can be either negatively or positively specified as [+ / - tense]. The tense features in a finite clause are [+ tense] whereas the tense features in a non finite clause (infinitivals and gerundivals) are [- tense]. In most languages, such as English, the [+ AGR] feature is present only in [+tense] clauses.

As stated earlier, languages differ in regard to whether the features of INFL are morphologically realized on the verb. In richly inflected languages such as Italian, German, and Spanish, the AGR features are realized on the verb in the form of overt inflections. In languages such as English and French, which do not have "rich" inflectional paradigms, the features of AGR are realized overtly for some verb forms but not for others. In languages such as Chinese, Japanese, and Malayalam, the features of AGR are never realized on the verb in the form of overt inflection.

The features of AGR and Tense (being affix features) need to be realized on a verbal head. Some languages such as English, allow lexical elements such as modals to be base generated in the INFL position. Therefore, when a modal is present, the modal takes on the features of AGR and Tense. In the absence of a modal auxiliary, if an aspectual auxiliary such as *be* or *have* or a copula *be* is present, the auxiliary verb/copula inside of VP raises to the INFL position to take on the features of Tense and Agreement. In languages such as Italian and Spanish, thematic verbs like auxiliary verbs can also raise to INFL position. However, in languages such as English, non-auxiliary verbs cannot move to INFL. So in those cases, where there is no modal or auxiliary, the INFL features are said to lower and attach themselves to the main verb.

The notion of Government is an important one in GB theory.The basic idea underlying the notion of government is that a "head" governs the elements within its maximal projection but not those elements which lie outside its maximal projection. Case (abstract Case) is assigned under government. The definition of Government (Aoun and Sportiche 1983) is given in (3) below:

3.  $\alpha$ governs $\beta$ iff $\alpha$ is a lexical category or Agr and for all $\gamma$, $\gamma$ a maximal category, $\gamma$ dominates $\alpha$ iff $\gamma$ also dominates $\beta$.

In GB theory, INFL which is the head of IP, is said to govern the subject position (the SPEC of IP position) to which nominative Case is assigned. The assignment of nominative Case to the NP in [SPEC, IP] is dependent on the positive specification of the Tense feature in INFL. INFL that is [-Tense] cannot govern the [SPEC, IP] position and does not have Case to assign to an NP in this position. Typically, therefore, (excluding Exceptional Case-marking structures in English such as, *I want [him to go there]* ), the only element that can occur in [SPEC, IP] of a tenseless clause is the empty category PRO, which must not be governed.

## 2.2. Null Subjects and Rich Agreement

As we saw above, the Extended projection principle states that every sentence must contain a subject position. Although the subject position is obligatory, languages vary with respect to whether the subject must be lexically realized or not. In pro-drop languages, overt subjects are optional and can be dropped from tensed clauses.[3] This is illustrated by the sentence from Spanish shown in (4a).

    4a.   Come     como una bestia
            eat-3rd per.sing. like a beast
            'Eats like a beast'

Although the subject is not lexically realized, the sentence in (4a) can be interpreted as having a definite pronominal subject (*pro* ). Sentence (4a) is equivalent to (4b) .

    4b.    El (ella)   come   como una bestia
            He (she)   eats    like  a    beast
            'He (she) eats like a beast'

In languages such as English and French, lexical subjects are obligatory. For example, the English equivalent for (4a) is ungrammatical.

As we have seen, referential subjects are optional in pro-drop languages. In addition, non-referential subjects (i.e. expletive subjects) are not present in pro-drop languages, as the sentences from Spanish shown in (5) illustrate.

    5a.    Esta lloviendo.
            Is   raining
            'It is raining'

      b.    Habia mucha gente.
            Were many  people
            'There were many people.'

English, on the other hand, which instantiates the [- pro-drop] value, requires overt expletive subjects (non-referential *it* and *there* ).

Although different explanations have been offered for the pro-drop phenomenon, it is widely held that the pro-drop phenomenon is related to properties of the INFL node. Rizzi (1982) has argued that the INFL in pro-drop languages differs intrinsically from the INFL in non-pro-drop languages. According to Rizzi, the INFL in pro-drop languages is a *pronominal* whereas in non-pro-drop languages it is not. Where INFL is a pronominal it assumes clitic-like (or lexical) properties. First, it takes on the syntactic properties of the subject by absorbing the Case and θ–role (thematic roles such as, agent, theme, experiencer) which would otherwise be assigned to the NP in [SPEC, IP] position. Second, as a clitic, INFL functions as a proper governor which licenses an [NP e] (i.e. the empty category *pro* ) in subject position which is assigned nominative Case and θ-role. In Government theory, only lexical categories are "proper governors" whereas non-lexical categories are not. The notion of proper government follows from the Empty Category Principle (ECP). The ECP is stated in (6).

6.   An empty category must be properly governed.

In Spanish and Italian for example, INFL is a proper governor since it has lexical properties and therefore a null-subject or *pro* is allowed. In English, on the other hand, INFL does not have lexical properties and therefore cannot be a proper governor. Hence, *pro* does not occur in English. In other words, the assumption is that the possibility of *pro* occurring in a language is directly related to whether its identity can be recovered from the verb agreement endings. In "richly inflected" languages such as Spanish and Italian, *pro* can be identified by the AGR features (person and number) which are morphologically realized on the verb. English, on the other hand, is not "richly inflected" and therefore *pro* is disallowed.

At this point we need to state that according to Rizzi and others (Borer 1983; Gilligan 1987) AGR features must include person markers as they are the only "real" identifiers. Verb forms which are inflected for gender and number alone, but not person cannot function as identifiers. It must be clarified, however, that AGR can only determine the "content" of *pro,* but cannot specify its *unique* reference. Hence it may be misleading to assume that the $\phi$ features in rich agreement languages are capable of identifying or recovering in entirety the identity of a null subject. What is identified by the $\phi$ features in these languages are the formal features of the subject but not its specific or unique reference which can only be recovered from the discourse.[4]

Before we go on to discuss the problems inherent in an analysis which equates pro-drop with "richness of inflection", we will briefly examine Hyams' (1983, 1986) version of the pro-drop parameter, namely, the AG/PRO parameter.

## 2.3. The AG/PRO Parameter

Central to Hyams' reformulation of the pro-drop parameter is that in null subject languages such as Italian, AG (that is, the features of person, number and gender located in INFL) is not only a pronominal but a special type of pronoun, namely PRO. Since PRO is ungoverned, it cannot receive case. In (7) for example, X can govern Y and Y can govern X depending on which element is the head. Only verbs, nouns, adjectives and prepositions and AG can function as the head.

7.
```
      Z
     / \
    X   Y
```

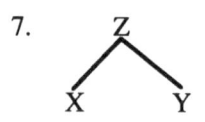

Hyams' proposals are essentially within the Government and Binding Model presented in Chomsky (1981), where, unlike in the Barriers framework, the X-bar theory of phrase structure had not been extended to the functional elements of INFL and COMP. Assuming that Z is INFL, X is AG and Y is AUX, if AG is PRO, PRO must not be governed. Therefore either AUX must be lexically empty or AG must not equal PRO. In English, which is a non-pro-drop language, AUX contains lexical material, such as modals and auxiliaries; AG in English is not PRO and can therefore be governed. In Italian and Spanish, which are pro-drop languages, AG is equal to PRO and cannot be governed. But PRO cannot be governed only if AUX is lexically empty. The absence of lexical material in AUX is accounted for by the commonly held analysis for modals and auxiliaries in Spanish and Italian. Auxiliaries and modals in these languages are not generated in AUX but as main verbs in VP since they exhibit many of the syntactic and morphological behavior of main verbs.

Hyams concludes that when AG=PRO, lexical material in AUX is excluded in any natural language. When AG is not =PRO, AUX can contain lexical material. Hyam's formulation of the AG/PRO parameter follows essentially in spirit Rizzi's formulation of the pro-drop parameter. Like Rizzi and others, Hyams assumes that there is a correlation between richness of inflection and pro-drop. However, Hyams' formulation differs from earlier analyses in that it attempts to relate apparently disparate elements namely presence or absence of pro-drop and absence or presence of lexical elements in AUX. Further, her analysis not only attempts to explain adult pro-drop and non-pro-drop languages, but also attempts to account for null subjects in child grammars. The role of the AG/PRO parameter in language acquisition is discussed in Chapter 3. We now turn to C.T.J. Huang's account of the null-subject facts in languages without agreement.

## 2.4. Null Subjects in Languages without Rich Agreement

As we saw above, according to most accounts, pro-drop can occur only in richly inflected languages. However, such an explanation is inadequate since it fails to account for the occurrence of null subjects in languages that are not inflected for person and number such as Chinese, Japanese, Malayalam and Korean. C.T.J. Huang (1984) argues that Chinese, Japanese and Korean are pro-drop languages. According to C.T.J. Huang, in these languages, only an empty category (EC) in the subject position of an embedded clause which can be coindexed with the subject of the matrix clause is *pro*. In other words, *pro* in Chinese, Korean, and Japanese can take as the potential antecedent the c-commanding nominal. The definition of C-command is given in (8).

8. $\alpha$ c-commands $\beta$ iff every branching node dominating $\alpha$ also dominates $\beta$ and $\alpha$ does not dominate $\beta$.

In the sentence shown in (9) from Chinese, the EC in the subject position of the embedded clause can be coindexed with the c-commanding nominal *Zhangsan* which is the subject of the matrix.

9. Zhangsan$_i$ xiwang [*e* $_i$ keyi kanjian Lisi]
   Zhangsan hope        can see      Lisi
   'Zhangsan$_i$ hopes that [he$_i$] can see Lisi.'

Likewise, in Japanese, an EC in subject position can be coreferential with its c-commanding nominal as in (10).

10. John-wa$_i$ [*e* $_i$ siken-ni otita] no-o mada siranai
    John        exam failed that    yet  not know
    'John$_i$ still does not know that [he$_i$] failed the exam.'

According to C.T.J. Huang, in addition to *pro*, Chinese, Japanese and Korean also allow empty categories in object positions. In Huang's formulation, empty categories in object position are distinguished from *pro* in these languages in that they cannot take a c-commanding nominal as a potential antecedent. Examples (11) and (12) illustrate this fact for Chinese and Japanese respectively.

11. *Zhangsan$_i$ xiwang [ Lisi keyi kanjian *e* $_i$]
    Zhangsan hope     Lisi  can see
    'Zhangsan$_i$ hopes that Lisi can see[him$_i$].'

12. *John-wa$_i$ [Bill-ga e $_i$ settokusuru] to omotte iru.
    John    Bill          persuade        that think
    'John$_i$ thinks that Bill will persuade [him$_i$ ].'

Similarly, in C.T.J. Huang's formulation, the EC in the subject position of the matrix clause in the Chinese sentence in (13) and the Japanese sentence in (14) cannot be considered to be *pro* because it is not locally bound by a matrix subject.

13. e  lai-le
       come-LE
       '[He/she] came.'

14. e  totemu isogashii desu
       very    busy      is
       '[He/She] is very busy.'

C.T.J. Huang refers to ECs in the object position (as in 11 and 12) and ECs in the subject position of a matrix (as in 13 and 14) as variables, which can only be bound by an NP in the discourse rather than in the matrix sentence. Following Tsao (1977), he argues that languages such as Japanese, Chinese, and Korean may be distinguished from languages like English by a typological parameter called *discourse-oriented* versus *sentence oriented*. In discourse oriented languages such as Chinese, Japanese, and Korean, there is a rule of *Topic NP deletion*. This rule applies at the level of discourse to " ... delete the topic of a sentence under identity with a topic in a preceding sentence. The result of such a deleting process is formally a *topic chain..*" (C.T.J. Huang 1984:549). The example cited by Huang and shown in (15) demonstrates Tsao's Topic NP deletion rule:

15. [Zhongguo, difang hen da.] [e, renkou hen duo.] [e, tudi
     China       place  very big    population very many   land
    hen feiwo.] [e, qihou ye hen hao.] [e, women dou hen
    very fertile  climate too very good        we    all  very
    xihuan.]
    like
    '(As for) China, (its) land area is very large. (Its) population is very big. (Its) land is very fertile. (Its) climate is also very good. We all like (it).'

Each of the ECs above represents the position of a deleted topic or what C.T.J. Huang calls as a variable. Thus, through the rule of topic chaining which operates in the discourse grammar of a discourse-oriented language, an empty topic node is coindexed with an appropriate preceding topic. Sentence-oriented languages, on the other hand, have a less substantive discourse grammar in that they lack this rule of topic chaining. As we will see, in section 2.6, this notion of identification through topic chaining plays an important role in Jaeggli and Safir's analysis of the null subject phenomenon.

To summarise, in discourse oriented languages such as Chinese, Japanese and Korean, only the EC which is in the subject position of a embedded clause is *pro*. All other ECs which occur either in the matrix subject position or in the object position are variables. Such ECs are identified by a topic or a possibly null sentence topic. While C.T.J. Huang's analysis accounts for the identification of ECs (*pro* and zero topics) in languages without agreement, it does not account for the facts of richly inflected languages such as German and Icelandic. Let us now turn to the theoretical construct of the MUP.

## 2.5. The Morphological Uniformity Principle

As we discussed earlier, the notion of rich agreement underlying earlier analyses of the null subject phenomenon is problematic when we consider that not all adult null subject languages have richly inflected verbal paradigms and that not all languages which are richly inflected allow null subjects. Jaeggli and Safir (1989) attempt to account for this problem by proposing a different approach to the null subject phenomenon. Central to their formulation is the notion of morphological uniformity. According to their formulation, null subjects are licensed only in languages with morphologically uniform verb paradigms. This requirement, which they term the "licensing condition" is stated in (16).

16. Null subjects are permitted in all and only those languages which have morphologically uniform inflectional paradigms.

A morphological paradigm is uniform if all its verb forms are morphologically complex or none of them are morphologically complex. The MUP is stated in (17) below.

17. An inflectional paradigm P in a language L is morphologically uniform iff P has either only underived inflectional forms or only derived inflectional forms.

According to Jaeggli and Safir, a word W belonging to a category K is 'underived' if it is morpologically non-distinct from the stem (or root) of W. A word W' belonging to a category K is considered 'derived' if it consists of a stem W plus an affix that is attached to W. The affix need not be restricted to prefixes, suffixes and infixes. In certain cases, other types of inflection may be present, such as suppletion, reduplication, stem vowel alterations or the insertion of appropriate vowels within consonantal skeleta.

Spanish and Italian observe the MUP and hence null subjects are allowed in these languages. All Spanish and Italian verbs are inflected for number, person, tense and mood and an uninflected verb is not possible. For example, the Spanish verb *hablar*, 'to speak' inflects in the present tense as shown in (18).

18. hablar

| habl-o | *I speak* | 1s |
| habl-as | *You (sg) speak* | 2s |
| habl-a | *he speaks* | 3s |
| habl-amos | *We speak* | 1pl |
| habl-ais | *you (pl) speak* | 2 pl |
| habl-an | *they speak* | 3pl |

Likewise, the Italian verb *parlare* 'to speak' inflects in the present tense as indicated in (19).

19. parlare

parl-o
parl-i
parl-a
parl-iamo
parl-ate
parl-ono

As we can see, in Italian and Spanish, each of the verb forms consist of a stem and inflection.

Japanese and Chinese, which are also null subject languages, have morphologically uniform verb paradigms. Japanese verbal paradigms inflect for tense/mood/aspect and negation but not for person and number as can be seen from the examples in (20). Chinese has no inflection affixation at all and an uninflected verb stem is the only possible form as (21) illustrates.

20.     yom-u     *read-present*
       yom-ta     *read-past*
       yom-eba     *read-conditional*
       yom-oo     *read-imperative*
       yom-itai     *read-volitional*
       yom-are     *read-passive*
       yom-ase     *read-causative*

21.     xihuan     *like*

English and French, which are non-pro-drop languages, are very different from Spanish, Italian, Chinese and Japanese. Unlike these languages, English and French have morphologically non-uniform or "mixed" verb paradigms. In other words, some of the forms are morphologically simple (i.e. they correspond to the stem) while others are morphologically complex. For example, as is illustrated in (22) for English, in the present tense paradigm for the verb *to talk*, only the third person singular form is inflected.

22.     to talk     infinitive
       talk     imperative [=stem]
       talk     present [ 1s, 2s, 1pl, 2pl, 3pl [=stem]
       talk-s     present 3s
       talk-ed     past
       talk-ing     gerund

Similarly, in French, some of the verb forms correspond to the stem while others do not as in (23).[5]

23.     [parl-e]     infinitive     *to speak*
       [parl]     imperative     2s[=stem]
       [parl]     present     1s, 2s, 3s, 3pl [=stem]

| [parl-ð] | present | 1pl. |
| [parl-e] | present | 2 pl |

Thus, according to Jaeggli and Safir, languages can vary in one of two ways with respect to the MUP. Languages can instantiate either the positive or the negative setting of the MUP. However, this overly simplifies the actual facts of inflection in languages, since in essence there are more than two choices: [-uniform] (e.g. English and French), [+uniform + inflected] (e.g. Spanish) and [+ uniform - inflected] (Chinese). As we will discuss in Chapter 3, the logical possibility of three choices poses certain problems in accounting for the facts of language acquisition within the framework of the MUP.

As stated earlier, some languages have morphologically uniform paradigms but do not allow thematic null subjects although they permit expletive subjects to be null. This is the case with verb second languages such as German and Icelandic. The verb forms in German, for example, are uniformly inflected for tense, person and number (and mood), although two or more forms may be identical in a given paradigm. Consider the present tense paradigm in German for the verb *arbeiten* 'to work'.

| 24. | (ich) | arbeit-e | *I work* | 1s |
| | (du) | arbeit-est | *you work* | 2s |
| | (er)/(sie) | arbeit-et | *he works* | 3s |
| | (wir) | arbeit-en | *we work* | 1pl |
| | (ihr) | arbeit-et | *you work* | 2pl |
| | (sie) | arbeit-en | *they work* | 3pl |

Despite the uniform verb morphology, German does not allow referential null subjects (see examples in 25). However, null expletive subjects are permitted as the sentences in (26) illustrate[6]:

25a. *...dass EC gegessen hat.
  'that   eaten has'

  b. * Gestern hat EC gegessen.
    'yesterday has eaten'

26a. ...dass EC in den Garten ein Kind gekommen ist.
  'that   in the garden   a child come has'

b. ...dass EC dem Kind geholfen wurde
'that the DAT child helped has'

c. Gestern wurde EC ein mann getotet.
'yesterday was a man killed'

The above examples from German indicate that the relationship between morphological uniformity and null subjects is not a direct one. To explain cases such as the above, Jaeggli and Safir propose an *identification requirement* which they distinguish from the *licensing condition* for null subjects. According to Jaeggli and Safir, morphological uniformity only licenses null subjects; in other words, it only states when a null subject is possible but not that it will in fact obtain. As we will see in section 2.6, the identification requirement is intended to explain when null subjects will actually occur.

As Jaeggli and Safir themselves state, it is not clear why morphological uniformity should be a licensing factor for null subjects. Furthermore, as Lillo-Martin (1991) has observed, several languages have different paradigms for the various tenses, moods, or aspects and it is unclear, given Jaeggli and Safir's proposals, as to which verb paradigm should be taken into account in determining whether the language is morphologically uniform or non-uniform. As Jaeggli and Safir have stated, the past tense paradigm in English has a morphologically uniform paradigm. Yet, null subjects are not permitted in English. Further, as Lillo-Martin (1991) points out, American Sign Language (ASL) has two types of verbs: derived verbs and underived verbs. Yet, in terms of Jaeggli and Safir's proposals, ASL should count as morphologically uniform since overt subjects are optional in ASL. An additional problem for Jaeggli and Safir's proposals is posed by the existence of morphologically mixed languages such as Bengali (J.Bayer's personal communication to Roeper and Weissenborn 1990), which nevertheless do allow pro-drop.

## 2.6. Identification of Null Subjects

The identification requirement follows from the θ-criterion (Chomsky 1981:36), which is given in (27). The θ-criterion constrains the mapping of θ roles (= thematic roles e.g. agent, theme, experiencer, goal, etc.) onto arguments (names, definite descriptions, pronouns, anaphors, and variables).

27. The θ-criterion
Each argument bears one and only one theta role

and each theta role is assigned to one and only one argument.

The identification requirement (Jaeggli and Safir 1989:32),which states exactly when null subjects will occur in a language, is defined in (28).

28. A thematic null subject must be identified.

In other words, if a predicate selects a subject to be thematic, i.e. to be assigned a θ-role, then a null subject will be barred whenever it is not identified, where identification is necessary for determining the referential value and referential value is crucial to the determination of the argument status of an NP. Therefore, a null subject language with thematic null subjects is a language which satisfies both the licensing condition of morphological uniformity and the identification requirement. On the other hand, languages with only expletive null subjects only need to satisfy the licensing condition as expletives do not have referential value.

Jaeggli and Safir propose two ways by which the thematic null subject can be identified. The first type of identification is identification by AGR. As stated earlier, it is a general consensus in GB theory that agreement affixes with the relevant φ-features (person and number features) are identifiers in languages such as Spanish and Italian. These features lie in the INFL node and they govern the subject position. The identification requirement (Jaeggli and Safir 1989:35) for null subject languages with rich agreement is stated in (29):

29. AGR-TENSE can identify an empty category as thematic *pro* iff AGR Case-governs the empty category.

In other words, the agreement features must be located in a category which also contains Tense, the feature which assigns nominative Case. Further, Jaeggli and Safir assume along with others (Rizzi 1982; Borer 1983; Gilligan 1987) that AGR features must include person markers as they are the only real identifiers. Forms which are inflected for gender and number alone, but not person cannot function as identifiers. In Spanish and Italian, the AGR features are located in INFL where Tense features are also located and so they meet the identification requirement.The requirement that AGR be contained in a category that Case governs the subject explains why verb second (V2) languages which are morphologically uniform, such as German and Icelandic, do not allow null thematic subjects. Following Platzack (1985), Jaeggli and Safir assume that in these languages the Tense features are located in COMP (or C of CP in Chomsky's (1986b) Barriers system ), that is, the second position to which the finite verb moves. Since the Tense features are not contained in the INFL node where the AGR features are located, the identification requirement is not fulfilled. Hyams (1992) represents the configuration for V2 languages as in (30).

30.  [COMP [+/-Tense] [$_S$ NP VP [INFL AG]]]

Since the thematic null subjects cannot be identified in verb second languages, the theory predicts that such null subjects will not occur in these languages. This is borne out in both German and Icelandic since both require obligatory referential subjects.[7]

The second type of identification obtains in languages such as Chinese and Japanese which uniformly lack person-number agreement. Following C.T.J. Huang (1984), Jaeggli and Safir assume that in these languages null thematic subjects of embedded clauses are identified by an overt c-commanding nominal. In addition to identification via the c-commanding nominal, Jaeggli and Safir assume that the null subjects are identified by a topic or possibly null topic. This idea stems from the distinction that C.T.J. Huang has drawn between "discourse oriented" languages such as Chinese and Japanese and "sentence oriented" languages such as English and French. As we saw earlier, "Discourse oriented languages" observe a rule of "topic chaining" which grammatically links the discourse topic to a null sentence topic, which in turn identifies a null argument. In C.T.J. Huang's analysis only the null subject of an embedded clause, which is identified by the c-commanding nominal, is considered as *pro* . On the other hand, the null argument (in subject or object position) which is identified by a null sentence topic grammatically linked to the discourse topic is considered as a variable. In Jacggli and Safir's modification of C.T.J. Huang's analysis (see also Jaeggli and Hyams 1988 and Hyams 1992), the null argument in the matrix subject position is also considered as *pro*.

The difference between null subject languages such as Italian and Spanish which are richly inflected and null subject languages such as Chinese and Japanese which lack agreement lies in the different methods that they employ for identifying the null subject. This difference is schematized by Hyams (1992:260) as in (31) below.

31.  a. Italian:
     [$_S$ pro$_i$   [$_{INFL}$ AG$_i$/Tense ] .....]
     b. Chinese:
     DISCOURSE TOPIC$_i$ [topic$_i$ [$_S$ *pro* $_i$ [ INFL ]....]

We mentioned earlier that in languages with rich agreement, the φ features can only indicate the formal features of subject and not its exact reference. In view of this, the inconsistency in Jaeggli's and Safir's proposals become apparent. In their framework, in languages such as Spanish and Italian, which are richly inflected languages, the method of identification is through agreement. However, in languages which are not richly inflected, such as Chinese and Japanese, the identification of the null subject is through the c-commanding nominal, the Topic or null sentence topic. Clearly the two types of identification are not on par since the two types are functionally different. In the case of Spanish and Italian, the features only provide the formal features of the subject, whereas, in the case of Japanese and Chinese, the unique reference of the null subject is recovered from the discourse. What their account fails to explain is what is common to both language types: unique reference recovered from the discourse.

Notwithstanding some of its problems, the theoretical construct of the MUP is of interest in terms of its implications for grammatical development in children particularly with respect to the use of null subjects and the acquisition of verbal inflections. Specifically, it predicts that null subjects are licensed only in those child grammars that are morphologically uniform (that is, where all or none of the verb forms are inflected). Further, it also predicts that null subjects will be realized only in those child grammars which satisfy the identification requirement. If null subjects are present in child grammars whose verb paradigms are uniformly uninflected or are uniformly inflected only for features other than agreement, we would expect the null subject to be identified by a Topic or a null sentence topic as in discourse oriented languages. If null subjects are present in child grammars which have uniformly inflected verb paradigms along with rich agreement markings, we would expect the null subject to be identified by the agreement features located in INFL.

## 2.7. Summary

In this chapter, we examined the properties of the INFL node which are considered to be related to the null subject or pro-drop phenomenon. Next we examined previous analyses of the pro-drop phenomenon and discussed their limitations. We then presented the theoretical construct of the MUP which has been posited by Jaeggli and Safir as a UG principle. Finally, we examined the Identification requirement which along with the MUP is intended to fully account for the presence or absence of null subjects.

In the next chapter, we will examine in detail the predictions of the MUP for language acquisition. In so doing, we will review previous research on the null-subject phenomenon in first and second language acquisition.

## Notes to Chapter 2

1. In casual speech in English, however, there is a tendency to omit a first person pronoun when it occurs at the sentence initial position as in the following sentences:

    > Flew in from Miami.
    > Think I'll go for a walk.

    However, such instances of subject omission are acceptable only in the sentence initial position of the matrix clause and subjects cannot be dropped from tensed embedded clauses.

2. Lydia White (personal communication) pointed out that in some recent analyses (Roberges 1986; Hulk 1987) French has been shown to be a pro-drop language. Central to the argument is the reanalysis of French subject pronouns as clitics.

3. It is a general consensus within GB theory that overt subject pronouns in pro drop languages such as Italian and Spanish are used only to convey contrast or emphasis. However, it has been shown (Duranti 1984) that Italian subject pronouns are devices through which speakers define main characters in a narrative and or convey empathy or positive effect toward certain referents. Inanimate objects, minor characters and people with whom the speaker is displaying lack of empathy or negative affect are instead often referred to by demonstratives. In addition, it has also been shown that in Turkish, which is a pro-drop language, overt subject pronouns are not only used for contrast and emphasis but also to initiate a change in topic (Enc 1986).

4. I am grateful to Mohanan (personal communication) and Swales (personal communication) for bringing this point to my attention. A similar point has also been made by Higginbotham (personal communication to C.T.J. Huang, cited in C.T.J. Huang 1984).

5. This, of course, applies only to spoken French since in written French the inflectional endings are preserved.

6. Gass (personal communication) stated that the German data are problematic since it is not evident that (26a) and (26b) do indeed have null expletive subjects. It may be argued that both sentences have overt referential subjects. The subject in (26a) is the nominative 'ein Kind' and the subject in (26c) is the nominative 'ein mann'. Only in (26b), where 'Kind' takes the dative case, is there a null expletive subject. The above interpretations were attested by two native speakers of German. Thus, the data in (26a) and (26c) are controversial. To data in (26b) we may also add other examples such as, *Heute abend wird getanzt* ('Tonight is dancing') where there is a clear case of a null expletive subject. However, it is relevant to mention that there are some cases in German where expletive subjects are obligatory. For example, the German equivalent for 'It is raining' is *Es regnet*. Although *Es* in this utterance is a non-referential (non-thematic) subject, its deletion would result in an ungrammatical sentence. In terms of Jaeggli and Safir's analysis, however, we would not expect this to be the case. However, if we assume that in the case of sentences such *Es regnet* involving weather predicates, the subject is quasi-argumental and not a true expletive subject, then such sentences do not pose a problem for Jaeggli and Safir's analysis as we would not expect a subject that is quasi-argumental to be omitted in German (but see note 7).

7. However, in German casual speech, referential null subjects reportedly occur but their occurrence is restricted to the sentence initial position (Ross 1982; Roeper and Weissenborn 1990 ).

# 3 Null Subjects in Developing Grammars

## 3.0. Introduction

Several scholars have argued that the null subject phenomenon is a universal property of child language ( Hyams 1983, 1986, 1992; Guilfoyle 1984; Jaeggli and Hyams 1988; O'Grady et al 1989; Weissenborn 1992 among others).[1] According to these arguments, there is an initial period in child L1 acquisition during which thematic (referential) lexical subjects are optional and lexical expletive subjects are entirely absent regardless of whether the target language is a null subject language or not. For example, the evidence from studies of the early grammars of null subject languages such as Italian (Hyams 1986; Valian 1991), ASL (Lillo-Martin 1991) and Chinese (Wang et al 1992) indicates that children acquiring these languages appear to understand from the very beginning that overt subjects are optional. As for the early grammars of English, which is a non null subject language, Hyams (1986) observed that children learning English as the L1 omit thematic and non-thematic subjects during the early stages. This is illustrated by the examples in (1) from Bloom, Lightbown and Hood (1975). The utterances in (1a) have null thematic subjects and those in (1b) have null expletive subjects.

1a. Want more apple
See under there
No play matches
Show Mommy that

1b. Outside cold ('It's cold outside')
Yes, is toys in there ('Yes, there are toys in there')
No morning ('It's not morning')

According to Hyams (1986, 1992) there is a subject-object asymmetry with respect to the omission of arguments in the early grammars of English. Subjects are often dropped but objects, on the other hand, are rarely omitted.

As in the case of English-speaking children, children learning French and German as the L1 appear to initially treat these languages as null subject languages as the examples in (2) indicate. The French examples in (2a) are from Weissenborn (1992) and the German examples in (2b) are from Clahsen (1986).

>2 a. Veux manger
>'(I) want to eat'
>
>Est sale
>'Is dirty'
>
>Est tombé
>'Has fallen'
>
>2b. Faellt um
>' (I) fall down'
>
>Dreht immer
>' (It) always turns'

Several explanations have been offered for the null subject phenomenon in the early grammars of non null subject languages such as English. According to one view, the omission of subjects in early English is a result of performance factors (e.g. L. Bloom 1970; Mazuka, Lust, Wakayama and Snyder 1986; P.Bloom 1990; Gerken 1990; Valian 1991). P.Bloom (1990) analyzed the CHILDES transcripts of Adam, Eve and Sarah and specifically suggested that subject omission is a function of VP length and not a result of an incorrect parameter setting. According to P.Bloom, lexical subjects in early English are typically longer than pronoun subjects and are more difficult to process than the latter. Likewise, pronoun subjects impose a greater processing load than null subjects. As a result, when a lexical or a pronoun subject is present, the processing resources that are available for the remaining part of the sentence are greatly diminished, which in turn results in a shorter VP. Valian (1991) compared the frequency of subjects produced by English speaking children and Italian speaking children and she found that the former group used subjects and pronoun subjects more than twice as often as the latter at the same developmental level. Based on her findings, Valian argued that English-speaking children appear to know that English requires obligatorily overt subjects before mean length of utterance (MLU) 2.0. According to Valian, since Italian is a null subject language, the Italian-speaking children are omitting subjects as a result of parameter setting whereas the English-speaking children are doing so because of performance constraints (for a review of performance based explanations, see Hyams and Wexler 1993).

In contrast to the proponents of performance based accounts of the null subject phenomenon, several scholars have argued that subject omission in early English is a result of a linguistic deficit. According to this view, during the initial stages, English speaking children do not yet understand that English requires overt subjects. According to one competence based account, English speaking children drop subjects because of the non-availability of certain aspects of Universal Grammar such as the Case Filter and functional categories such as INFL (Guilfoyle 1984; Radford 1990). Another particularly interesting proposal is that English speaking children initially omit subjects because of an initial parameter setting that is consistent with a null subject language such as Italian or Chinese (Hyams 1986, 1992; Jaeggli and Hyams 1988). In what follows, we will examine the parameter setting accounts proposed by Hyams and Jaeggli in detail before addressing the issue of the status of subjects in SLA.

### 3.1. Parameter Setting Accounts of the Null Subject Phenomenon

Hyams (1983, 1986) proposed a version of the pro-drop parameter, namely the AG/PRO parameter. As we saw in Chapter 2, in pro-drop languages AG is considered to be PRO; hence, there can be no lexical material in AUX, for otherwise PRO would be governed. In non-pro-drop languages AG is not equal to PRO and therefore lexical material can appear in AUX. According to Hyams, the early grammar of English differs from adult English in its value for the AG/PRO parameter. In the early grammars of English, as in the early grammars of all non-pro-drop languages, AG is identified as PRO. Hence, these early child grammars exhibit many of the properties of pro-drop languages such as Italian and Spanish. Referential subjects are optional and expletive subjects are entirely absent. Further, lexical material such as modals and auxiliaries are entirely lacking. When the child realizes that in English, AG is not equal to PRO, subjects become obligatory and lexical material appear in AUX. Thus, in this analysis, the emergence of subjects is considered to be directly related to the development of modals and auxiliaries. According to Hyams, this change in the child's grammar from optional subjects to obligatorily overt subjects is triggered by the child's perception of expletive subjects *it* and *there* in the input.

Hyams (1992) discusses some of the problems with the above analysis. A major problem relates to the identification of the null subjects in the early grammars of English. In her 1983 and 1986 analysis Hyams argued that children learning English move, as it were, from a stage when they treat English as a pro-drop language, like Italian, to a stage when they treat English as English (i.e. non-pro-drop). In Italian, the identity of the null subject can be recovered from the verb agreement endings. This appears to be true for the early grammars of Italian as well. As Hyams (1983, 1986, 1992) has stated, Italian speaking children acquire verb morphology much earlier than English speaking children. Hence, the subjectless utterances in the early grammars of Italian *are* pro-drop utterances since the identity of the null subjects can be recovered from the verb inflections. But this method of identification is not possible in the early grammars of English. As Hyams (1992) observes, English speaking children use null subjects despite the fact that verbal morphology, such as it is in English, is not acquired at this point. Thus Hyams' (1983, 1986) analysis of the null subject phenomenon within the framework of the AG/PRO parameter violates the identification requirement of the null subject. If we assume this framework, we would have no other alternative but to argue that the subjectless utterances observed in the early grammars of English are not really pro-drop utterances and may have an entirely different explanation.

Hyams (1992), Jaeggli and Hyams (1988) offer an alternative to the 1983 and 1986 null subject analysis, which is intended to overcome the above problem. Their alternative analysis is based on the notion of morphological uniformity proposed by Jaeggli and Safir (1989). As we may recall, the MUP predicts that null subjects will be licensed in those child grammars that are morphologically uniform but not in those grammars that are not morphologically uniform. It further predicts that null subjects will be realized only in those child grammars which fulfill the identification requirement. If the child's language is richly inflected, then the null subject will be identified through AGR (as in Spanish and Italian). If the child's language is not richly inflected then, the null subject will have to be identified through a Topic or null sentence topic as in Chinese. Jaeggli and Hyams attempt to show that in early child language, morphological development and null subjects are related.

In the following sections, we first examine Hyams and Jaeggli's arguments for the relationship between the development of verb morphology and null subjects in child L1 acquisition. Specifically, we discuss some of the weaknesses in their account of the null subject phenomenon. Next, we discuss the predictions of the MUP for SLA and we review recent studies of the null subject phenomenon in L2 grammars of English. In so doing, we focus on a study by Hilles (1991) and a preliminary study by Lakshmanan (1991) which tested the predictions of the MUP in the context of SLA.

## 3.2. Morphological Development and Null Subjects in Early Grammars

According to Jaeggli and Hyams (1988) and Hyams (1992), the occurrence of null subjects in early grammars is a result of the child's initial assumption that the language is [+ uniform]. This claim makes a number of predictions about early child L1 acquisition. For example, let us consider a child acquiring English, which is a [-uniform] language. In terms of Jaeggli and Hyams' claims, the following would be the predicted developmental stages:

(i) Null subjects will occur in the initial stages.
(ii) Either all or none of the verbs will be inflected.
(iii) Once the child realizes that English is not uniform, null subjects will be abandoned.

To test the above predictions, Hyams (1992) analyzed data on Adam from Brown's (1973) longitudinal acquisition study. She found that the data on Adam support these predictions. There is an initial period when subjects are optional and verb inflections are omitted. When target-like past and present inflectional patterns emerge, that is when the child realizes that English is morphologically mixed, null subjects are abandoned.

According to Jaeggli and Hyams, although all children go through a period of null subjects, their early grammars will vary with respect to the method by which null subjects are identified. For some children, the identification will be through topic chaining and for others the identification will be through agreement. The choice of one identifier as opposed to another will be determined largely by the properties of the language being learned. Thus in their analysis, since English speaking children initially omit inflections, the null subject in the early grammar of English is identified by a Topic or possibly null sentence topic (as in Chinese). Children learning English, in their view, move from a stage where they treat 'English like Chinese' to a stage where they treat 'English like English'.[1]

Jaeggli and Hyams observe that verb morphology is acquired more quickly by children acquiring languages which are morphologically rich, such as Italian (see Hyams 1986) and Polish (Weist and Witkowska-Stadnik 1985) than it is by children acquiring a morphologically non-uniform language such as English, where verbal inflections are acquired very late (Brown 1973). In order to account for this variation, they propose that the child's initial or default setting is that the language is morphologically uniform (either all the verb forms will be inflected or none of the verb forms will be inflected). Those languages that fulfill this expectation will be easier to acquire than those that do not.

Jaeggli and Hyams observe that there is no theory internal reason why [+ uniform] should be the initial parameter setting. However, they claim that from a learnability-theoretic perspective, the initial setting of [+ uniform] is the more restrictive hypothesis. Consider, for example, a child learning a language which is [ - uniform]. If the child's initial assumption is that the language is [+ uniform] that is, that all the verb forms are inflected or none of the verb forms are inflected, positive evidence will indicate that the language is [- uniform]. On the other hand, if the child initially assumes that the language being learned is [- uniform] when in fact it is not, no number of inflected or uninflected tokens will suffice to change the initial analysis (since the child cannot be sure whether the next form he/she hears will be an uninflected or inflected form).[2] As Jaeggli and Hyams observe, their proposals for the initial setting of [ + uniform ] follows from the Subset Principle, which we discussed in Chapter 1. A language which is [ + uniform ] is considered to be a smaller language than a language which is [- uniform]. The latter includes both inflected and uninflected forms whereas the former has only inflected forms or only uninflected forms. The child's initial hypothesis, in their view, would be consistent with the smaller language. The subset principle with respect to the MUP may be schematized as in Fig. 3.1.

NULL SUBJECTS IN DEVELOPING GRAMMARS 53

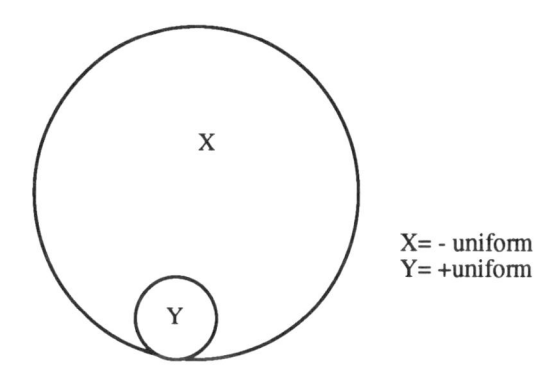

X = - uniform
Y = +uniform

*Fig. 3.1: Subset Principle with respect to the MUP*

While Hyams and Jaeggli's proposals are attractive in terms of the precise predictions that are offered, their analysis is not without its share of problems. Firstly, the MUP predicts that there should be no stage in child grammars of [ - uniform] languages in which the irregular verb inflections are acquired and subjects are still absent. Data from the early grammars of French and English disconfirm this prediction. As Weissenborn (1992) has shown, French children continue to omit subjects long after they have correctly analyzed that spoken French is a [-uniform] language, that is, when past and present inflections emerge. This is illustrated by the examples in (3).

3. a fait
'has made'

va chercher un avion
'going to look for a plane'

est tombé
'has fallen'

Ai tout bu le verre moi
' Have drunk the whole glass me'

Ai mangé des quettes (= crepes)
'Have eaten pancakes'

Ça marche pas
'That doesn't work'

Evidence from children's spontaneous revisions of their prior utterances also appears to weaken Hyams and Jaeggli's claims. Shatz and Ebeling (1991) examined the home conversations of six English children (from the age of 2;0 to 2;6) and found that child-initiated revisions of their own prior utterances were extremely frequent. While such revisions were primarily at the semantic and phonological level, there were also many syntactic revisions which involved the addition or deletion of subjects and verbs. An analysis of these child-initiated revisions revealed that although there was a trend toward improved grammaticality, there were many revisions which resulted in less grammatical utterances. Further, a "wavelike pattern of improvement and decrement" rather than a straightforward linear trend was observed with respect to such revisions. Moreover, the improvement in the grammaticality of revisions was gradual rather than sudden. Hyams and Jaeggli's model predicts that subjectless utterances will be abandoned as soon as verb inflections are acquired. However, Shatz and Ebeling's findings suggest that subjectless utterances are neither abruptly nor entirely abandoned when verb inflections are acquired. The change from optional subjects to obligatory subjects, if anything, appears to be a gradual one. They observe that children who revise by adding and deleting subjects at 2;0 continue to do so at 2;6, although the percentage of such revisions has slightly reduced and the quality of the revisions has changed subtly. In terms of Jaeggli and Hyams' claims, revisions may be predicted to be used solely for adding subjects. However, as Shatz and Ebeling observe, many revisions involving the deletion of subjects were also present.

A second problem concerns the initial or default setting of the MUP. An outcome of adopting a notion of morphological uniformity is that languages where all the verb forms are inflected are treated as equal (in terms of the subset principle) to those languages where none of the verb forms are inflected. Thus, depending on the language, the child's initial assumption will be that either all the forms are inflected or none of the forms are inflected. For example, we would not expect a children learning Chinese to initially assume that Chinese is uniformly inflected since they would never hear an inflected form. However, the scenario for a child learning Italian or Spanish, which have uniformly inflected verb paradigms, is more complicated than the MUP predicts. A child acquiring Italian, for example, would never hear an uninflected form. Yet we cannot assume that the Italian child's initial hypothesis is that Italian is uniformly inflected. It has been observed that children learning Italian first tend to use the third person singular, present indicative form of the verb (e.g. *Mangia* 'eats') as the unmarked form (Bates 1976). In fact they extend this form even to cases where the subject referred to is the child herself/himself. In many of these cases, the child refers to herself/himself by name and therefore the third person singular marking would be acceptable for such sentences (e.g. *Caddia dorme* 'Claudia sleeps'). However, there are also other instances (although undoubtedly fewer), when the child makes mistakes--that is, uses the unmarked third person form of the verb when the subject is the first person singular pronoun. Thus, Italian speaking children at the initial stage cannot be credited with having correctly analyzed the third person form of the verb as consisting of a stem + inflection. A more valid explanation is that they may initially assume that none of the verb forms is inflected. Once the different verb endings are perceived as inflections and are mapped on to the relevant features (AGR, Tense etc.), they will reanalyze Italian as being uniformly inflected. However, the different verb endings are not learned all at once but have to be learned gradually. Therefore, there would be nothing to prevent the child from going through a stage where it assumes that Italian is a "mixed language" since the child uses an unmarked form (unmarked at least with respect to its current grammar) for several cases and an inflected form in other cases. During this stage, we would expect the child to supply overt subjects even when they would be unacceptable in the adult language. The problem is that in terms of Jaeggli and Hyams' proposals, no amount of positive evidence will be sufficient to force a reanalysis that Italian is [+uniform]. However, we know that children learning Italian do come to master the verb morphology of Italian, and, as Jaeggli and Hyams observe, they do this faster than children acquiring English. Jaeggli's and Hyams' proposals fail to account for the possibility that Italian children may initially assume that in Italian none of the verb forms are inflected and, further, that they may go through a 'mixed' stage (with some forms inflected and some forms uninflected) before correctly analyzing Italian as an uniformly inflected language.[3] Their suggestion that the Italian child's initial assumption is that it is uniformly inflected ignores the problem of accounting for the possibility of a 'mixed' stage. In light of the above, it would be reasonable to assume that the child's initial hypothesis is that the language is uninflected. The subset principle with respect to verb morphology would be more appropriately represented as in fig. 3.2 rather than as in fig. 3.1 above.

X = - uniform
Y = +uniform, +inflected
Z = +uniform, -inflected

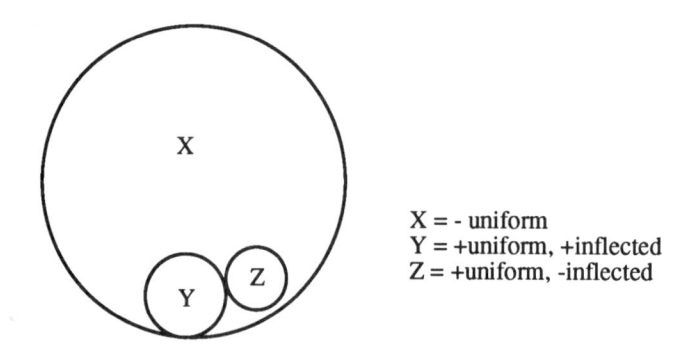

*Fig. 3.2: Revised Subset Principle with respect to the MUP*

From the discussion above, it is evident that the child is in fact presented with three choices: [+ uniform] [ + inflected], [+ uniform] [- inflected], and [- uniform]. The availability of these three choices, as opposed to merely two choices (i.e. [+ uniform] and [- uniform]), makes the facts concerning the development of inflections incompatible with an account that assumes a super-set/subset relationship between two languages, since a language which is [+uniform] [-inflected] cannot be characterized as a subset of a language that is [+ uniform] [- inflected] and vice versa. Perhaps it would be more valid to conceive of the variation among languages with respect to morphological uniformity as a sort of continuum (see fig. 3.3). This would more effectively account for the facts of inflection acquisition in the early grammars of Italian.

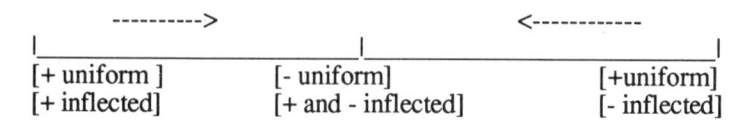

```
         ---------->                        <------------
|_____|_____|
[+ uniform ]           [- uniform]             [+uniform]
[+ inflected]          [+ and - inflected]     [- inflected]
```

*Fig. 3.3 : Continuum of Verb Inflectional Paradigms*

Another problem concerns Jaeggli and Hyams' claim that the null subjects in the early grammars of English are identified through a Topic or a null sentence topic as in Chinese. Jaeggli and Hyams fail to substantiate this claim with data from the transcripts of the longitudinal study (Brown 1973) that they examined. One type of evidence for their claim would be the existence of topic-comment structures such as for e.g., *Salt, I taste it in this food* or, alternatively: *I taste it in this food, salt..*[4] As Brown (1973, 131-132) has stated, there are 'fewer than a dozen instances' of topic comment structures in the same data that Hyams and Jaeggli considered. Two such are *Shadow, go get it* and *Daddy suitcase, go get it* from Adam (stage I). On the other hand, as Brown observes, 'there are thousands of sentences that seem to be subject predicate constructions' (p. 132). While topic comment structures and subject predicate structures could conceivably coexist, we would expect there to be more of the former than the latter. However, this does not seem to be supported by the data. Thus, if we accept Hyams' and Jaeggli's proposals regarding the identification of null subjects, we would have to explain away all the numerous instances of subject predicate constructions in order to maintain the topic-comment sentence as the norm.

Let us assume that Jaeggli and Hyams' account of missing subjects in the early grammars of English is indeed correct, and that the initial hypothesis entertained by English-speaking children is that English is like Chinese. As discussed in Chapter 2, the adult grammars of Chinese not only permit the omission of subjects but of objects as well. If English-speaking children treat English like Chinese, we would expect them to drop not only subjects but also objects. However, as Jaeggli and Hyams observe, although English speaking children omit subjects they rarely omit objects. In order to account for the subject-object asymmetry, Hyams (1992) argues that in the early grammar, the inventory of null elements includes *pro* but not variables. A major piece of evidence that Hyams cites for the absence of variables during the initial stage is based on Roeper, Rooth, Mallis and Akyama's (1984) finding that children appear to violate strong crossover for a long period of time (but see McDaniel and Mckee (1992) for evidence that English-speaking children do not violate strong crossover and that variables are present in early English). As discussed in Chapter 2, according to C.T.J. Huang (1984), only an empty category in the subject position of an embedded clause that can be coindexed with the subject of the matrix clause is *pro*. Under C.T.J. Huang's analysis, the empty category in subject position of a matrix clause and the empty category in the object position are not instances of *pro* but are zero or null topics (i.e. variables). Hyams (1992) departs from Huang's proposals regarding the status of null elements in Chinese and suggests that an empty subject of a matrix clause and an empty subject of an embedded clause are both instances of *pro* although the method of identification is different for each of these two types of empty subjects. *Pro* in the matrix subject position is identified by a discourse topic whereas *pro* in the embedded subject position is identified through coindexation with a c-commanding NP.

Assuming that null objects are variables, Hyams' proposals would account for the subject-object asymmetry in the early grammars of English. At the same time, however, we would also expect to observe a similar subject-object asymmetry in the early grammars of Chinese. In their recent study, Wang et al (1992) found that Chinese speaking children omit a greater number of subjects than English speaking children. In addition, they found that Chinese speaking children also omitted objects, which is contrary to what Hyams' proposals would predict. Following Lillo-Martin (1991), Wang et al propose that there is more than one parameter involved in the omission of arguments in adult grammars. One parameter, whose positive value is instantiated in languages with rich agreement such as Italian, is the Null pronoun parameter and the element *pro* in these languages is identified through Agreement. According to Wang et al, the null arguments in discourse oriented languages such as Chinese are a result of an entirely different parameter, namely the Discourse-Oriented parameter (DOP). The null arguments in Chinese type languages can be classified into one of two types: The null arguments in matrix subject position and object position, which are identified by a Discourse topic, are variables while the null argument in the subject position of an embedded clause, which is identified by a c-commanding NP is the element *pro*. Wang et al propose that the initial setting of the DOP is [-DO]. According to Wang et al, Chinese-speaking children will encounter overwhelming positive evidence that Chinese is a discourse oriented language and they will correctly reset the value of the DOP to [+DO]. As a result, they will omit both subjects and objects as in the case of the adult grammars of Chinese. Assuming that [-DO] is the default setting as Wang et al claim it is, we would not expect English speaking children to omit subjects. Wang et al assume following Hyams' that there is a grammatical basis for subject omission in the early grammars of English and they appear to rule out performance based accounts of the null subject phenomenon in early English. Specifically, they claim that English speaking children omit subjects because of the Null pronoun parameter and not because of the DOP and that the Null pronoun parameter is initially set at the positive value as in Italian. However, their claim is problematic in view of the fact that the identity of the null subjects in early English cannot be recovered through Agreement because of the absence of verb inflectional morphology. In contrast, the null subjects in the early grammars of richly inflected languages such as Italian, can be easily recovered because of the presence of overt agreement markings on the verb. An alternative to Wang et al's proposals would be that the initial setting of the Null pronoun parameter is (as in the case of the initial setting of the DOP) also consistent with a negative value. If this is indeed the case, then we would have to conclude following Valian (1991) and P.Bloom (1990) that English speaking children do indeed know that English requires overt subjects but that they sometimes omit subjects because of performance factors.

An issue that poses a problem for Hyams and Jaeggli's parameter setting account of the null-subject phenomenon is the presence of contradictory data in the input that the child is exposed to. Valian (1990) points out that English speaking children are exposed to subjectless sentences, which can mislead them into thinking that English is a null subject language. Examples of misleading input include imperative sentences such as *Wash yourself*, which are grammatical and also sentences such as *Want your lunch now* and *Raining hard* which are acceptable in the contexts uttered but not fully grammatical. As Valian (1990) observes, an acquisition theory will have to account for how, English-speaking children, for example, come to know that overt subjects are obligatory in English despite the presence of contradictory data. While Jaeggli and Hyams do not address this issue, Roeper and Weissenborn (1990) discuss the problem posed by such contradictory data for learnabiliy theory and argue that the parametric approach is essentially correct, but that it is in need of refinement. In the case of the null-subject parameter, they observe that English-speaking children may encounter missing subjects in matrix clauses, but not in tensed embedded clauses. In other words, the subordinate clause functions as a unique trigger in that it does not contain any ambiguous information. Unlike the matrix clause, the evidence is consistent with only one of the parametric choices. The task for the child is to discover the unique trigger. Such knowledge, as Roeper and Weissenborn claim, is not part of UG, but is a part of an acquisition device which is used by the child in analyzing the data in the input. In her recent study, Valian (1991) found that English speaking children do not omit subjects in tensed embedded clauses, thus lending support for Roeper and Weissenborn's proposal that the subordinate clause has a unique triggering function.

## 3.3. Predictions of the MUP for SLA

Despite the difficulties with Hyams and Jaeggli's claims, let us assume the MUP and consider it within the context of second language acquisition of morphologically non-uniform languages such as English. We saw in Chapter 1 that there are three logical possibilities with respect to L2 learners' access to UG namely, direct access, indirect access, and no access. Let us first consider the predictions of the MUP with respect to the direct access scenario. We may recall that in the direct access situation, the L2 learner is believed to have access to the original switch box settings (including default settings) without the interference from the L1 settings. Assuming that the MUP is a UG principle, then regardless of whether the L1 setting is [+ uniform] or [- uniform], we would expect L2 learners of English (and other morphologically mixed languages) to initially assume that English is [+ uniform]. Thus, we would expect L2 learners of English to go through the same stages as has been claimed for children acquiring English as L1. These stages are presented below.

(i) They will assume that English is morphologically uniform.
(ii) Inflections will be absent.
(iii) There will be an initial period of null subjects.
(iv) When present and past inflections emerge (i.e. when they realize that English is morphologically mixed), null subjects will be abandoned.

Let us now turn to the indirect access scenario. As stated in Chapter 1, in the indirect access scenario, many or all of the principles will be set in L1 terms. If the L1 setting differs from that in the L2, resetting (using principles of UG and on the basis of positive evidence from the L2) will be carried out resulting in a reorganization of the IL grammar that is consistent with the facts of L2. In the indirect access scenario, we would expect only those learners whose first languages instantiate the [+ uniform] setting to go through the above stages. They will initially transfer the setting of [ + uniform] to the L2 . Then during the reorganization phase, the mapping of the L1 setting will be revised within the definite confines of the MUP and on the basis of positive evidence from the L2. Learners with a [- uniform] L1 will be expected to transfer the setting of [-uniform] to the L2. However, although they will transfer the setting of [-uniform] to English, they will still need to work out the language specific facts of L2 as in the case of the learners from a [+ uniform] L1 background. In other words, they will still have to figure out which of the forms in a given verb paradigm are inflected and which forms correspond to the stem. At the same time, because of the initial assumption that English is [- uniform], we would expect them to acquire the past and present inflections of English much earlier than learners from a

[+ uniform] first language background. As a result, we would not expect their IL to include null subjects.

Finally, let us consider the "no access to UG" scenario. As we discussed in Chapter 1, according to the no access to UG position, the learners do not have access to UG principles. Instead, the L1 will function as an initial template and the L1 settings will be mapped directly onto the L2. Hence, the learners' IL in situations where the L1 settings match the L2 parameter settings may be misleading in that they may suggest that UG is still active. However, situations where the L1 settings differ from the L2 settings will serve to clarify that UG is no longer available. In the absence of UG, parameter resetting cannot take place. Instead, the L2 learner may have to resort to inductive learning mechanisms or other general learning principles in learning the L2, which as we saw earlier, will result in certain non-natural features occurring in the IL. In terms of the MUP, we would expect the L2 learners to directly transfer the setting with respect to morphological uniformity from the L1 to the developing L2. Null subjects may or may not occur in the learners' IL, regardless of whether the [+ uniform] or [- uniform] setting is instantiated in the L1. Even if null subjects occur, we would not expect decreases in null subjects to be related to the development of verb inflections since the phase of reorganization would be absent. As we observed in Chapter 1, the conclusion that child L2 learners do not have access to UG can only be validly maintained on the assumption that the MUP is indeed a UG principle.

## 3.4. Null Subjects in Developing L2 Grammars

The null subject or pro-drop phenomenon has received considerable attention in SLA research (Zobl 1984; White 1985b; Phinney 1987; Hilles 1986; Lakshmanan 1986; Liceras 1988). All of the above studies are based on earlier formulations of the pro-drop parameter.[5] Two recent studies that specifically tested the predictions of the MUP are those of Hilles (1989, 1991) and Lakshmanan (1991). It is of interest that the two studies arrived at different findings even with respect to the IL of the same subject. In what follows, we first review Hilles' study and discuss some of its methodological problems. Next, we briefly present the findings of the preliminary analysis reported in Lakshmanan (1991) which suggest that the development of verb inflections and the null subject phenomenon are unrelated.

Hilles (1989, 1991) examined the IL of six Spanish speakers (two children, two adolescents and two adults) acquiring English as L2. The purpose of her study was to investigate whether development of verb morphology and emergence of subjects were related in these subjects' IL. The transcripts of the IL of six subjects from the longitudinal SLA study by Cazden, Cancino, Rosansky and Schumann (1975) were used for the purpose. Hilles found that only the two children (Marta and Cheo) and one of the adolescents (Jorge) had access to the UG principle of MUP whereas the two adults (Alberto and Dolores) and the other adolescent (Juan) did not. In other words, Hilles found that development of verb morphology and emergence of subjects were highly correlated in the IL of Marta, Cheo and Jorge but not in the IL of Juan, Alberto and Dolores.

There are several methodological problems with Hilles' study. First, the fact that increases in inflections and increases in subjects are highly correlated does not indicate that there is a causal relation between the two, as predicted by the MUP. It may be that these aspects, like other aspects of language development, happen to emerge at the same time (particularly when it is an increase in something that is presented in the IL). Secondly, Hilles' findings may be the result of the method adopted to calculate the percentage of null subjects in each subject's IL. Hilles' method for calculating the percentage of null subjects is the same as the one used in her earlier study (Hilles 1986). The formula used for calculating the percentage of null subjects was as follows:

$$\frac{X}{Y + X}$$

(Where X = number of actual instances of null subject, and Y= number of cases where null subjects could have occurred but did not)

In order to calculate the Y cases, Hilles took into account discourse factors. Therefore, the Y utterances in her study included only those instances where the identity of the referent had been clearly established in the discourse.[6] In other words, according to Hilles, the Y cases represented those tokens of subjects which would have been dropped had the text been in Spanish that is, where the identity of the null subject had clearly been established in the discourse and could be recovered from the verb endings. There are several problems with this method. Firstly, Hilles assumes that the L2 learners will transfer the discourse strategies in Spanish to English. However, as Hilles has stated, verb in-

# NULL SUBJECTS IN DEVELOPING GRAMMARS

flections are omitted in the early stage. Hilles uses this as evidence to argue that the null subjects are identified through topic chaining as in Chinese; so on the one hand, in order to calculate the percentage of null subjects, Hilles assumes that the discourse strategies in Spanish are transferred to English (even though null subjects cannot be identified through agreement, there being no agreement). At the same time, Hilles states that null subjects are identified as in Chinese. The problem is that there is no data available on any of the subjects which can tell us about their use of the discourse rules of Spanish. Perhaps for the adult and adolescent learners, one can assume that they have mastered these rules. But for the two children, it is not at all clear whether they are in fact using the discourse rules of Spanish. An outcome of Hilles' method is that the value of the denominator (the sum of Y+X) used to calculate the percentage of null subjects is lower than would otherwise have been obtained had only syntactic factors been taken into account and as a result, the proportion of null subjects is greatly overestimated. If, on the other hand, the Y cases had consisted of those utterances where there was a subject and a verbal element (either a main verb or auxiliary) and where it would be clearly incorrect in English to delete the subject, then this would have increased the value of the denominator (the sum of Y+X) and the proportion of null subjects thus computed would have been smaller.[7]

A third problem is that Hilles does not take into account factors of the input. There is evidence from the data that the learners (in particular Cheo) have received input suggesting that English is a null subject language (for a discussion of this issue, see Chapter 5). Fourth, although Hilles' study suggests there is a strong correlation between increases in verb inflections and increases in subjects, she does not present any statistical evidence to show that development actually takes place with respect to increases in subjects.

A fifth problem concerns inflection acquisition. It is a well known fact that in first and second language acquisition, the various inflectional morphemes are not acquired at the same time. However, Hilles considered all the different categories of verb inflections (copula, third person singular, auxiliaries be, have and do ) together and did not examine the relationship between the development of each of the sub-categories and emergence of subjects.

Finally, Hilles' study does not provide sufficient evidence that the learners for whom there appears to be a significant correlation between inflection acquisition and null subjects do in fact have access to the default setting of the MUP and are not merely transferring the setting from the Spanish L1. Hilles argues that at the initial stage, the null subjects in Marta's, Cheo's and Jorge's IL are Topic identified as has been argued by Hyams and Jaeggli for the early grammars of English. Some of the evidence that she cites in support of her claim is the use of the accusative form of the pronoun as a subject pronoun, and the occurrence of topic/comment utterances.[8]

    4.    Her is sleeping    (Marta 05/11)
           Him, him he like, he no like to play with crayons.
                  (Cheo 7. 19/08)
           My school it have water in there    (Cheo 7/21.05)

Thus, according to Hilles, the early IL of Marta, Cheo and Jorge is of the Chinese type, where the closest, and the only identifier is the Topic. In other words, they are said to treat English as a *discourse oriented* language. Hilles further argues that when AGR emerges as a category, the three subjects go through a middle stage when there are two competing identifiers, Topic and AGR. According to Hilles, during this stage, the condition of the closest identifier comes into play and the subjects are forced to choose between the two identifiers. Since the closest one in this case is AGR, AGR is selected. In other words, during the middle stage, the subjects assume that English is like Italian-that is, a sentence oriented language with null subjects. Once it is apparent that agreement is not uniformly present in English, null subjects are abandoned.

A problem with the above analysis is that on the basis of a very few occurrences of topic/comment structures, null subjects are claimed to be identified through topic chaining as in Chinese. Assuming that Hilles' arguments are indeed valid, we would expect to find topic-comment utterances even in the earliest samples, where in terms of her analysis the percentage of null subjects is very high. However, there are no clear instances of topic comment utterances in the early samples for Marta, Cheo and Jorge. Further, the existence of such topic/comment utterances may at best be regarded as indirect evidence that the Spanish speaking subjects have access to the default setting of the MUP. What is needed is evidence from the early stages of the IL of speakers of a -null subject language such as French. Since Hilles did not consider native speakers with a -null subject L1, her findings that Marta, Cheo and Jorge have direct access to the MUP, and therefore to UG are inconclusive.

Lakshmanan (1991) carried out a preliminary analysis of the IL of three children Marta (a native speaker of Spanish), Muriel (a native speaker of French), and Uguisu (a native speaker of Japanese), all of whom were acquiring

English as a second language. The data on Muriel were obtained from Gerbault (1978), the data on Uguisu were obtained from Hakuta (1975) and the data on Marta were obtained from the study by Cazden, Cancino, Schumann and Rosansky (1975), that is, the same data that was used by Hilles. The purpose of the study was to test the predictions of the MUP. Unlike Hilles' study, this preliminary analysis did not find any evidence that development of verb morphology and decreases in null subjects are related in the IL of these subjects. In the case of Marta, who was also one of the subjects considered in Hilles' study, the phonological matching between English *it's* and *is* and the Spanish copula *es* appeared to trigger the + null subject setting from Spanish. However, this does not appear to have serious consequences. Null subjects occurred largely in *is* (copula and auxiliary) contexts and except for the very first sample, the percentage of null subjects was very low compared to what was obtained by Hilles for this same subject. This is probably related to the differences between the methods adopted in the two studies. A detailed discussion of these differences is presented in Chapter 4. In the case of Muriel, it was found that nearly all the null subjects are restricted to *it is* constructions and do not generalize to other verbs/pronouns. Null subjects in Muriel's IL appear to be the result of her efforts in analyzing *Its* and unlike in the case of Marta's IL, null subjects fluctuate until the very last samples. In the case of Uguisu, her IL had hardly any null subjects. In order to measure inflection acquisition, the simple presence/absence of tense inflection (Past regular *-ed*) and agreement (present 3rd singular *-s* and present 3rd singular irregular- *has* and *does* ) were taken into account. The overall picture with respect to the acquisition of these inflectional morphemes in the case of Marta and Muriel is that they are not acquired even in the last few samples. In the case of Uguisu, the regular morphemes (past *-ed* and 3rd singular *-s*) never reach the 80 % criterion for acquisition. In contrast, the irregular morphemes (*doesn't* and *has*) are acquired earlier by this subject.[9,10]

Since this was a preliminary analysis, not all the different categories of the inflectional morphemes were considered. Further, statistical measures were not applied to test for the significance of the results. Thus, although the study did not find evidence in the subjects' IL that development of verb inflections and emergence of subjects are related, the results cannot be regarded as conclusive.

In view of the major differences between the findings of Hilles' study and our preliminary analysis, a question that needs to be posed is: What are the implications of these findings for the MUP? Hilles found strong evidence in support of the posited relationship between acquisition of verb inflections and use of null subjects in the case of three of her subjects. Assuming that SLA data can provide an important testing ground for specific theoretical claims, Hilles' findings suggest that the MUP is indeed a UG principle. In contrast, the findings of our preliminary study (even with respect to the same subject that Hilles considered) suggest that claims for a universal status for the MUP are questionable. We noted that the contradictory findings may have been the result of the methodological differences between the two studies. It may be argued that it is merely a question of 'how one chooses to paint a picture'. However, such an argument would only fail to address the issue of the role of UG in SLA. The contradictory findings of the two studies, serve to indicate the pressing need for a reevaluation and refinement of SLA research methodology. For otherwise, it will be difficult to validly maintain our beliefs that SLA data provide a forum for evaluating linguistic theory.

## 3.5. Summary

In this chapter, we examined Hyams and Jaeggli's analysis of the null subject phenomenon in child language and discussed some of the problems inherent in their analysis. We suggested that the default setting in terms of real time acquisition is [+ uniform - inflected] rather than [+ uniform]. We discussed some of the problems that this poses (in terms of the subset principle) for the early grammars of Italian. In addition, we also questioned Hyams' and Jaeggli's claims that null subjects in the early grammars of English are identified through topic chaining as in Chinese. We examined the evidence from the early grammars of Chinese, which renders weak the argument that English-speaking children initially hypothesize that English is like Chinese. We also discussed the issue of contradictory data, which is not considered by Hyams and Jaeggli in their account of the null subject phenomenon in early English. Next, we discussed the predictions of the MUP for SLA. We then discussed the findings of Hilles' (1991) study and we examined some of its methodological problems. Finally, we presented the findings of a preliminary study which suggest that the MUP and the null subject phenomenon may not be related. In the following Chapter, we present the findings of a more detailed follow-up study.

## Notes to Chapter 3

1. Hyams (1992) examines the data from Clahsen (1986) on the early grammars of German and concludes that early German is a null subject language. During this stage, the predominant word order is SOV, even in the case of simple clauses where the correct adult order is SVO. Thus, at this point, null subjects are both licensed and identified since tense features are in INFL along with the agreement features. However, when the early grammar of German shifts from SOV to the correct word order SVO in simple clauses, null subjects decrease dramatically. Hyams argues that when this restructuring takes place, Tense is situated in COMP, and since Tense and agreement are no longer contained in the same node, the identification condition is blocked. The problem with this analysis is that while it accounts for the absence of null subjects in simple clauses with SOV word order, it does not explain why German speaking children do not omit referential subjects once they are able to produce embedded clauses (since the word order in the embedded clause in German is SOV).

2. White (personal communication) pointed out that Jaeggli and Hyams' argument that changing from an assumption of [-uniform] to [+uniform] would be impossible from a learnability perspective would be valid only if there were infinite numbers of inflectional paradigms in a language. But given the fact that the paradigms are quite limited, even if the initial assumption were that the language is [- uniform], the child could easily discover that the language is [+uniform].

3. Evidence from child second language acquisition of Spanish also suggests that the various verb endings are learned gradually. Dato (1970) examined the development of the Spanish verb phrase in the IL of six children, all of whom were native speakers of English. All the children initially used the third person singular indicative form of the verb as the unmarked form. This form is first used in imperative constructions (e.g., *Dispara! pinta!* ). This easily leads to the formation of an utterance in the third person since the only structural change involved is a change in the intonation (*Dispara una bala* '(He) shoots a bullet'). Next, the second person singular form in the declarative emerges, which involves the addition of final -s as in *Tu disparas a este* 'You're shooting this time'. This is followed by the first person singular form as in *yo disparo* 'I shoot'. However, as Dato has observed this form alternates with the inappropriate inflection -a as in *\*yo dispara* or *\*yo pinta*. Thus, there appears to be evidence that these children do not initially hypothesize that Spanish is uniformly inflected. There is also no evidence that they have correctly analyzed the third person form of the present indicative as an inflected form. Further, during the time when they first begin to use the appropriate inflection for the first person they also overgeneralise the third person form to this context. In other words, like the Italian speaking child, these learners also appear to move from a stage when they assume that there are no inflections to a stage when some forms are inflected and others are not.

4. Gruber (1967) examined the early grammar of an English speaking child (Mackie) and claimed that his early sentences were of the topic-comment type rather than the subject predicate type. For a critique of Gruber's position, see Brown (1973)

5. While the null subject phenomenon in IL is a well attested fact, the role of cross-linguistic influence in subject pronoun deletion is not fully clear. Although there is plenty of evidence to suggest that such deletion takes place in the English L2 of Spanish and Italian speakers, it has also been argued that such deletion is not confined to those speakers whose L1 exhibits the property of pro-drop. Zobl (1984) reports systematic pronoun deletion in L1 French learners of English and argues that subject pronoun deletion occurs regardless of whether pro-drop is allowed in the L1 or not. Further, Zobl has stated that null expletives are more persistent than null referential pronouns. White (1985b) investigated the pro-drop parameter in adult L2 acquisition. The subjects were L2 learners of English and consisted of a Spanish speaking experimental group and French speaking controls. The subjects were required to make grammaticality judgments on several English sentences, including some with pro-drop properties, which are ungrammatical in English. White sought to determine whether the following properties associated with the pro-drop parameter (as formulated by Rizzi, 1982) would transfer to the interlanguage of her subjects: missing subjects, V-S order in declaratives, and *that* -trace violations. White found that the Spanish speakers carried over the pro-drop parameter from the L1 to L2, while the French controls did not. Lakshmanan (1986) replicated White's study with subjects from different pro-drop L1 backgrounds (Spanish, Arabic and Japanese). The findings of this study did not entirely support White's findings. Specifically, the dramatic improvement with increasing levels of proficiency observed by White was supported only in the case of the Arabic speakers but not in the case of either the Spanish or Japanese speakers.

Hilles (1986) used Hyams' (1986) framework of the AG/PRO parameter to examine the extent to which some aspects of English IL restructuring by a 12 year old Spanish speaking learner could be the result of resetting the value along the AG/PRO parameter from AG= PRO ( i.e. + pro-drop) to AG is not equal to PRO ( i.e. - Pro-drop), and whether the change in the setting is triggered by the initial acquisition of several concomitant properties, namely expletive *it* and a lexically realized AUX. Hilles found that pro-drop is present in early IL but diminishes with time. In addition, she found that pro-drop in Jorge's IL decreases with the emergence of lexical material in AUX. Hilles also found some evidence that suggests that expletives may act as a trigger for the resetting from [+.Pro-drop) to [- Pro-drop); however, the evidence for expletives as triggering data is far from being conclusive.

Data from English speakers learning Spanish as L2 is considerably sparser compared to data from Spanish speakers learning English. Phinney (1987) examined production data (in the form of free compositions) of Spanish students learning English and English speakers learning Spanish. Phinney found that Spanish students have long-lasting difficulties with subject pronoun usage in English, supporting her hypothesis that going from an unmarked setting of the pro-drop parameter to a marked version is difficult for the L2 learner. On the other hand, the English speakers learning Spanish appeared to reset the parameter comparatively quickly. Liceras (1988) reports on a study involving two French and two English speaking adults, acquiring a pro-drop language (Spanish). Liceras' study is based on Rizzi's (1982) formulation of the pro-drop-parameter. She found that the subjects had fully acquired the property of null subjects but not the other properties associated with this parameter, namely V-S word order in declaratives and *that*--trace.

6. It is not evident from Hilles' study whether the X cases were analyzed for whether they were appropriate deletions of the subject i.e. whether they are identifiable. If this was not done, as Shatz (personal communication) has pointed out, it is another methodological flaw.

7. For example, in the case of Marta, Hilles found the percentage of null subjects to be 90% in sample 1, and 80% in sample 2. Subsequently, the percentage of subjectless utterances dropped to around 45% in sample 3 and gradually decreased to around 20% in sample 7. For this same subject, our preliminary study found the percentage of null subjects to be only around 64% in sample 1 and in the next sample, the percentage of null subjects dropped to around 16%.

8. O'Grady (1991) questions Hilles' assumption that the objective pronoun in the sentences in (4) functions as a topic rather than a subject. He cites Kaper's (1976) observations that the child's choice of the accusative form could simply reflect an overgeneralization on the part of the learner rather than the use of a topic-comment construction. As O'Grady points out, the objective case is unmarked in English and occurs in several structural contexts while the nominative form, which has only one use (marking the subject), is the marked form.

9. As Hakuta (1974) has stated, the relatively early acquisition of the irregular morphemes may be related to the fact that a root change is involved which makes them more salient than inflectional endings.

10. Hyams and Safir (1991) in their review of Lakshmanan's (1991) study make a distinction between passive knowledge and active knowledge and claim that a child may know whether the target language is morphologically uniform or non-uniform without being able to produce the individual forms that the uniform or non-uniform grammar includes. According to Hyams and Safir, Lakshmanan's finding that the use of English inflection by the three child L2 learners of English failed to reach the criterion, even thought they stop omitting subjects (as in the case of Marta and Muriel) or never omit subjects (as in the case of Uguisu), does not provide any evidence against the MUP since it could well be that they may have determined that English is not uniform but may merely not have mastered all of the inflections. Hyams and Safir suggest that in the case of Muriel and Uguisu, who went through a silent period lasting for a few

months, the generalization that English is not uniform could have been arrived at even before the onset of production. In other words, according to Hyams and Safir, the three child L2 subjects probably knew more about English than is evidenced in their productions. A problem with Hyams and Safir's proposals is that while they avail of the distinction between passive knowledge and active knowledge in accounting for the use of English inflection by the child L2 subjects, they do not use the same criteria in the case of subject omissions in the early grammars of English. Using their own arguments, it could well be the case, as Valian (1991) and P.Bloom (1990) have proposed that the presence of null subjects in early English does not accurately reflect children's knowledge about the status of overt subjects in English. That is to say, English-speaking children may be aware that English requires overt subjects but may merely fail to obey this requirement in their actual productions because of performance constraints.

# 4 Morphological Uniformity and Null Subjects in Child L2 Grammars

## 4.0 Introduction

As discussed in Chapter 3, the MUP makes certain precise predictions for second language acquisition. It predicts that the occurrence of null subjects in the IL of L2 learners acquiring English, which is a [- uniform] language, is related to the acquisition of verb inflections. L2 learners will initially assume that English is [+ uniform] and hence null subjects will occur. When past and present inflections emerge, that is, when the learners realize that English is [- uniform], null subjects will be abandoned. However, we saw in Chapter 3 that our preliminary analysis of the IL of three children learning English as a second language did not offer any direct evidence in support of these predictions. In contrast, Hilles (1991) found evidence in support of the predictions of the MUP, even with respect to the same subject, namely Marta. We discussed the possible reasons for the differences between the findings of these two studies. As we saw earlier, one of the major reasons may be related to the differences in the methods used to calculate the percentage of null subjects. Further, our preliminary study examined the occurrence of null subjects in *is* contexts versus *non-is* contexts whereas Hilles did not. A third reason may be related to the fact that unlike Hilles' study, our examination of inflection acquisition was restricted to a few inflectional types (present third person singular regular, present third person irregular *has* and *does*, and past regular *-ed*).

In this chapter, we report on the results of a larger and more in-depth analysis, and one which is intended to remedy some of the shortcomings of our preliminary study.

## 4.1 Research Questions

The present research tested the predictions of the MUP in the IL of four child subjects, Marta, Cheo, Muriel, and Uguisu, all of whom were acquiring English as a second language. In so doing, the following research questions were addressed with respect to the relations between null subjects and verb inflections.

i. Do null subjects in the IL of these child L2 learners decrease with time?
ii. Is there a developmental relation between null subjects and verb inflections in the IL of these child L2 learners? In other words, is increase in verb inflections accompanied by a corresponding decrease in the use of null subjects?
iii. Are obligatory verb inflections acquired at the same time for all the categories of verb morphology or does the acquisition of verb inflections depend on the specific category of verb morphology (e.g. the copula *be*, auxiliaries *be*, *do*, *have*, present third person singular regular, past regular etc.)?[1]

In addition to the above research questions which are driven by the theoretical construct of the MUP, the following questions, which were derived from the findings of our preliminary study, were also addressed. Specifically, these research questions deal with the developmental and non-developmental relations between the context (*is* context /*non-is* context) and type of subjects (null subjects / lexically realized subjects).

iv. Is there a developmental relation between null subjects in *is* constructions (*is* copula and auxiliary utterances) and *is* constructions? In other words, does the proportion of null subjects present in *is* contexts increase with the increase in the proportion of *is* constructions?
v. Are there any differences between the distribution of null subjects and subjects in *is* constructions and *non-is* constructions in these child L2 learners' ILs?

## 4.2 Methods

In order to address the above questions, transcripts of the IL of the four child subjects, Marta (a native speaker of Spanish), Cheo (a native speaker of Spanish), Muriel (a native speaker of French) and Uguisu (a native speaker of Japanese) were examined. The transcripts of Marta's and Cheo's IL were obtained from the longitudinal study by Cazden, Cancino, Rosansky and Schumann (1975); The transcripts of Muriel's IL were obtained from the longitudinal study by Gerbault (1978) and the transcripts of Uguisu's IL were obtained from Hakuta (1975).

### 4.2.1 Subjects

All the four subjects, Marta, Cheo, Muriel and Uguisu were acquiring English mainly through exposure to the English speaking environment. The data on Marta and Cheo were part of a larger project on the second language acquisition sequences of six Spanish speaking subjects (two children, two adolescents and two adults) reported in Cazden, Cancino, Rosansky and Schumann (1975). The data on Muriel, the native speaker of French, were reported in a longitudinal study by Gerbault (1978) which examined this subject's acquisition of interrogative and negative structures and grammatical morphemes. The data on Uguisu, the native speaker of Japanese were reported in a study by Hakuta (1975) which investigated Uguisu's acquisition of grammatical morphemes. The chief characteristics of the four subjects are described in Table 4.1.

*Table 4.1: Subjects' Characteristics*

*Marta*

Four and a half year old female from Puerto Rico; native speaker of Spanish; daughter of a professional couple-- at time of study, father was a graduate student at Harvard University. The duration of the study was approximately seven and a half months. Marta had been in the U.S. for one month before the study began. Prior to coming to the U.S., Marta had attended nursery school in Puerto Rico which was taught in Spanish, but had some English speaking children attending. She had also attended summer camp for six weeks which was conducted in Spanish but had some English speakers attending. She did not receive any formal instruction in English in the U.S. and her ability in English at onset of the study included some limited comprehension of simple English phrases and a few English words (mainly nouns). Spanish was the language primarily spoken at home. At the time of the study, Marta was attending an all English nursery school.

*Cheo*

Five year old male from Colombia; native speaker of Spanish. Father was doing graduate work at Harvard medical school. The duration of the study was approximately eight and a half months. Cheo had been in the U.S. for around four months before the data were collected. He had had no previous exposure to English and did not receive any formal instruction in English in the U.S. His ability in English at the beginning of the study was none and he did not produce any English during the first month of the study (that is, the period when the first two samples were collected). Spanish was the main language spoken at home. At the time of data collection, Cheo was attending an English speaking kindergarten.

*Table 4.1: Subjects' Characteristics (contd.)*

---

*Muriel*

---

Four and a half year old female from France; native speaker of French. daughter of a professional couple; mother was a graduate student in Applied Linguistics at UCLA. The duration of the study was approximately 11 months. Muriel had been in the U.S for 3 months before the data were collected. She had had no previous exposure to English and did not receive any formal instruction in English. Muriel did not produce any English for the first three months before the onset of the study. French (the L1) was spoken mainly at home and sometimes at the French-English bilingual school that Muriel was attending. During the first three months of her stay in the U.S., Muriel attended an English speaking nursery school. Subsequently, she began to attend a French-English bilingual school. Muriel mainly used English when communicating with her peers at school and also at home.

---

*Uguisu*

---

Five year old female from Japan; native speaker of Japanese. Daughter of a professional couple; father was a visiting scholar at Harvard for two years. The duration of the study was 15 months. Uguisu had been in the U.S. for two months prior to the onset of the study. She had had no previous exposure to English and did not receive any formal instruction in English in the U.S. Uguisu went through a "silent period" for the first three months of the study and did not produce any English during this period. Japanese was mainly spoken at home. Uguisu first attended an English speaking nursery school and later attended first grade. She used English when communicating with her American friends.

---

## 4.2.2 The Data

As Cazden, Cancino, Schumann and Rosansky (1975) have reported, Marta and Cheo were observed approximately every two weeks and speech samples were recorded in three situations: spontaneous speech recordings, elicitations, and preplanned sociolinguistic interactions. Marta was observed for a period of seven and a half months and Cheo was observed for a period of eight and a half months. Thus, the corpora consist of a total number of fifteen samples for Marta and a total number of ten samples for Cheo. As stated in Table 4.1, Cheo did not produce any English when the first two samples were obtained; hence, sample 3 represents Cheo's first attempts at producing English.

In the first type of situation, spontaneous speech was recorded as it occurred naturally in conversation, with the experimenter as participant observer. The second type of situation, namely elicitations, consisted of two types: elicited conversations and experimental elicitations. The elicited conversations were obtained using two instruments: the Bilingual Syntax Measure (Burt, Dulay, Hernandez-Chavez 1975) and the Ilyin Oral Interview (Ilyin 1972). Both the instruments elicited speech through a set of pictures and a series of questions about the pictures. In addition, elicited conversations were generated through the use of other pictures (e.g. magazines) and games. Experimental elicitations were used to get the subject to produce certain linguistic structures. The methodology for this type of data collection is based on the techniques used for the study of first language acquisition by Brown and Berko (1960) and Slobin (1967) among others. Experimental elicitations involved imitations, translations, transformations etc. For the purposes of the present research, only the data obtained through spontaneous speech recordings and elicited conversations were considered. The data obtained through experimental elicitations were not included. This was done in order to ensure that the data for the Spanish speaking subjects were more in line with the data that were available for the other two subjects, which did not include any experimentally elicited utterances.

The data on Muriel consists of seventeen samples. As Gerbault (1978) has reported, there was no systematic planning of taping sessions. The investigator, that is Gerbault, was the subject's mother, and therefore in the subject's immediate environment; thus, she was able to record data whenever there was verbal communication. Hence, a few of the samples include speech gathered at more than one time. However, each of the samples approximately corresponds to a two week period. Nearly all the speech data collected were generated in natural situations with the subject interacting spontaneously with either her mother or more usually with one of her American peers. The exceptions to the naturalistically generated data consisted of two administrations of the Bilingual Syntax Measure. Experimental elicitation tasks designed to get the subject to produce specific linguistic structures, such as imitations, translations, and transformations were not used.

As Hakuta (1975) has reported, Uguisu was observed for at least two hours every two weeks for a period of fifteen months. Thus a total number of thirty samples were obtained of which the first twenty samples were considered for the purposes of the present research.[2, 3] The data on Uguisu consist of spontaneous speech data recorded in naturalistic situations. The early samples

MORPHOLOGICAL UNIFORMITY AND NULL SUBJECTS 77

(samples 1 - 6) were obtained during Uguisu's interactions with her peers in play situations. The subsequent speech samples were obtained in situations where the subject interacted spontaneously with the experimenter. As Hakuta has stated, prior to the first sample, that is, after three months of exposure to English, several attempts were made to gather data, but Uguisu produced little speech. Although it would have been possible to elicit speech from her at the time by plaguing her with questions, Hakuta chose to let her begin speaking in a natural environment, which was a play situation with her peers. Thus, the first sample represents her earliest attempts at production.

*4.2.3 Data Analysis*

The transcripts of the IL of the four subjects, Marta, Cheo, Muriel, and Uguisu were examined for their use of null subjects and verb inflections. In what follows, we report on the various procedures adopted in analyzing the data of these subjects. The method adopted to calculate the percentage of null subjects while similar in some respects to the method used by Hilles (1986, 1991), differed from her method in certain crucial ways. As in Hilles' study, only non-imperative utterances were considered for the analysis. Further, the following types of (non-imperative) utterances were not taken into account: (i) Formulaic utterances, such as *I don't know, How are you*.[4] (ii) Utterances involving missing subjects plus auxiliaries and (iii) utterances where it would be acceptable in colloquial English to omit the subject in sentence initial position. Some examples of (ii) are given in (1a) and (1b) and an example of (iii) is shown in (1c):

(1) a. Experimenter (E) : What are you doing?
 Marta: Kratch, kratching. ( scratching)
 (Marta, Sample 12)
 b. E: What are the boy and girl doing here?
 Cheo: Putting the boot.
 E: Putting on the boots.
 (Cheo, Sample 5 )
 c. Feels sticky.
 (Uguisu , sample 8)

The formula used to calculate the percentage of null subjects was as follows:

$$\frac{X}{Y + X}$$

(Where X = number of actual instances of null subjects and Y= number of cases where null subjects could have occurred but did not.)

The percentage of null subjects included cases of referential null subjects as well as expletive (non-referential) null subjects. Some examples of expletive null subjects are given in (2).

(2)   Is not hot now.              (Marta, sample 9)
      I know is some more.         (Muriel, sample 16)

A major methodological difference between Hilles' (1986, 1991) study and the present study is that in order to calculate the Y cases, discourse factors were not taken into account in this study. Therefore, the Y cases consisted of those utterances where there was a lexical realization of a verb/auxiliary and where it would be incorrect in English if the subjects were deleted. This is illustrated by the examples in (3) where it would be ungrammatical to delete the subjects. For the sake of clarity, the relevant subjects in the utterances are italicized.

(3)   a.   *This* is Sesame street.         (Marta, sample 3)
      b.   *This* is a mother. *The mother* is going to eat.
                                            (Marta, sample 5)
      c.   *My teacher* has a book, and *I* go to hear the book.
                                            (Marta sample 8)

This method was preferred to Hilles' method for the following reason. It was considered more reliable, as it was not evident, for example, from the data on Marta, whether she was using the discourse rules of Spanish in her English. As stated in Chapter 3, our preliminary analysis of the data on two of the subjects (Marta and Muriel) suggested that null subjects were either largely restricted to or occurred more frequently in *is* contexts as opposed to *non-is* contexts. This factor could not be taken into account if Hilles' method had been adopted.

In addition to calculating the percentage of null subjects in each of the samples, null subjects occurring in *is* contexts (*is* copula and *is* auxiliary contexts) were separated from those occurrences of null subjects in *non-is* contexts.

Likewise, subjects supplied in *is* contexts (including *'s* contexts) were separated from subjects occurring in *non-is* contexts.

The method used to measure inflection acquisition was similar in some ways to that reported in Hilles, but differed from her method in certain other respects. In English, overt marking for tense and/or agreement is weakly realized on the copula *be*, auxiliaries *be*, *do* and *have*, present third person singular regular, present third person irregular (*has* and *does* (main verbs), past tense (regular) form of the verbs, and modals.[5] The absence of tense and/or agreement was considered as base, indicating the uninflected base form of the verb or auxiliary.[6]

The transcripts for each of the subjects were examined for the presence or absence of the overt coding of tense and/or agreement. This involved two main procedures. The first procedure involved the setting up of the target criterion for overt marking for tense and/ or agreement. In order to accomplish this, I asked the following questions of each utterance. The first question was: Would there be overt coding for tense and/or agreement in English? If the response to this question was 'yes', the next question was: How would this coding be overtly realized in the context of the utterance? In other words, would the coding involve the use of the copula, auxiliaries *be*, *do*, *have*, third person singular regular, or past regular etc.? Thus the obligatory inflections for the different types of verb morphology were established (As stated in Chapter 3, Hilles (1991) did not separate the obligatory uses of inflections in terms of the different types of verb morphology). A negative response to the first question indicated that the verb in the utterance examined would be uninflected in English.

The second procedure involved posing the following questions for each of the utterances for which the previous procedure had indicated that there should be overt coding for tense and/or agreement in English. The first question was: Is there overt coding for tense and/or agreement? If the answer to this question was 'yes, there is overt marking for tense and / or agreement', then the verb in the utterance in question was coded as an inflected form. If overt marking was not present, then the verb in the utterance in question was marked as an uninflected or base form. If overt marking for only tense was present (where the target criterion required that both tense and agreement should be coded), then the verb/auxiliary was considered as a base form. This was necessary because the presence of overt marking for only tense (where overt marking for both tense and agreement are required) would not be an indication that a given paradigm has been analyzed as morphologically mixed. Instead, this would be evidence that the learner treats English as a morphologically uniform language. For example, consider the present tense paradigm for the auxiliary *do* in English. The third person singular form *does* is overtly coded for both agreement and tense whereas the other forms in this paradigm indicate the tense features (i.e. present tense) but not the agreement features. Thus, if the learners use *do* where *does* is required, this would be an indication that they are treating the present tense paradigm for the auxiliary *do* as uniform rather than non-uniform. The second question that was posed of the inflected form was, 'How is the marking for tense and/or agreement lexically realized? Is it an instance of a copula, or auxiliaries *be*, *have*, *do*, or present third person singular etc.? Thus, the exact lexical realization of the overt coding was also noted. However, the target language was not considered as the yardstick for inflection acquisition. Credit was given for a particular inflected form regardless of whether it lexically matched the form in the target language. This was done because of the following reason. As we may recall, the MUP's predictions are that null subjects will be abandoned when present and past inflections (such as they are in English) emerge. The MUP does not predict that null subjects will decrease only when the verb inflections lexically match the target inflections. In other words, the overt realization of tense and agreement features where the target criterion dictates as being necessary (regardless of whether these overt realizations lexically match the target forms or not) would be an indication that the learner has realized that English is a morphologically mixed language.

The above procedure may be illustrated with a few examples. Consider, for example, the utterances in (4), which are taken from the transcripts of two of the subjects, Marta and Uguisu:

(4) a. He *eat* persons.
(He (the monster) eats people) (Marta, sample 7)
b. My grandfather he *cry* when I go to this here.
( In the context : My grandfather cried when I left Puerto Rico) (Marta, sample 3)
c. Is it feel good ?
( Does it feel good ?) (Uguisu, sample 8)

In (4a), Marta has failed to inflect the verb *eat* for agreement where it is required. In (4b), the verb *cry* is not inflected for past tense. Both these verbs are therefore considered as uninflected or base forms. In (4c), we notice that

Uguisu has overt marking for tense and agreement (although her lexical choice that is, the auxiliary *is*, does not match the target). The utterance in (4c) is therefore considered as containing an inflected form.

The above analysis generated twenty-two subcategories/ subtypes which were combined to form nine major inflectional categories. These categories (and subcategories) are listed in Table 4.2. The total number of inflected forms supplied by each subject in each of the samples was obtained by summing the total number of inflected forms for each of the categories. The total number of obligatory inflections in each of the samples was obtained by adding together the total number of inflected forms and the total number of uninflected (base) forms. The proportion of the total number of inflected forms to the total number of obligatory uses of inflections was computed. In addition, the proportion of inflected forms to the total number of obligatory instances of inflected forms was calculated separately for each of the nine categories.

Table 4.2: *List of inflectional categories and subcategories*

|    | Category | Subcategories |
|----|----------|---------------|
| 1. | Copula | Is, Am, Are, Was, Were |
| 2. | Auxiliary *be* | Is, Am, Are, Was, Were |
| 3. | Auxiliary *do* | Do, Does (includes doesn't), don't, did, didn't |
| 4. | Auxiliary *have* | Have, Has |
| 5. | 3rd singular regular (- s) | |
| 6. | *Has* (main verb) | |
| 7. | *Does* (main verb) | |
| 8. | Past regular (- ed) | |
| 9. | Modals | |

The number and percentage of null subjects and the number and percentage of inflected forms (total inflections and inflections for each category) for each of the four subjects are presented in the Appendices to this Chapter.

## 4.3. Results

In this section, we discuss the results in terms of our research questions. In section 4.3.1., we present the findings with respect to the relations between null subjects and verb inflections. In section 4.3.2 we present the findings with respect to the relations between null subjects and *is* contexts.

### 4.3.1. Relations between Null subjects and Verb Inflections

This section is organized as follows. First we present the results of the analysis which examined whether null subjects in the four child L2 learners' IL decrease with time. Second, we present the results obtained for the analysis which examined the relationship between null subjects and verb inflections. Finally, we discuss the findings of the analysis which verified whether the use of verb inflections is related to the specific category of verb morphology.

#### 4.3.1.1 Null subjects

In order to investigate whether the null subjects in the IL of the child L2 learners decrease with time, logistic regression (see Cox 1970) was done on the number of null subjects and the session/sample number. Logistic regression was carried out separately for each of the four subjects. The results of the logistic regression analyses are presented in Table 4.3.

*Table 4.3: Results of Logistic Regression of Null Subjects and Time*

| Subject | Regression Coefficient | Significance |
|---------|------------------------|--------------|
| Marta   | $\beta = -.23964$      | $p < .00001$ |
| Cheo    | $\beta = -.18522$      | $p = .0034$  |
| Muriel  | $\beta = -.52059 -1$   | $p = .0039$  |
| Uguisu  | $\beta = -.34604$      | $p = .0060$  |

Logistic regression analyses showed that the development over time with respect to use of null subjects was statistically significant for all four subjects suggesting that all of them use fewer null subjects later than earlier ($p < .00001$ for Marta and $p < .01$ for Muriel, Cheo and Uguisu). Although statistically significant results were obtained for Uguisu, the results are not of practical significance for this subject as we will demonstrate below. When we examine the results for the other three subjects, we notice that the β value obtained in Muriel's case is the smallest. This suggests that the effect of time on the occurrence of null subjects in Muriel's IL is less compared to Marta and Cheo.

Let us now examine the evidence from the IL of each of the four subjects. Figure 4.1. shows the percentage of null subjects in Marta's interlanguage.

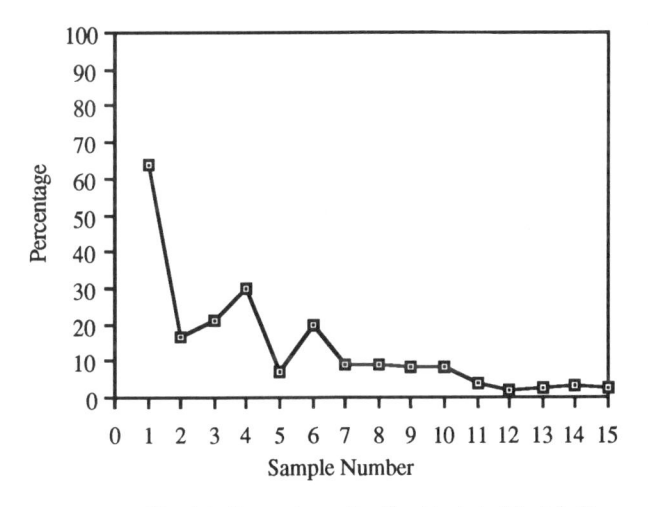

*Fig. 4.1: Percentage of null subjects in Marta's IL*

As we can see from Figure 4.1, null subjects occur around 64 % of the time in sample 1. There are hardly any pronouns (except for one case of *she/they*), and also no cases of *this*. In the second sample, the percentage of null subjects drops sharply to around 17% and increases to 30% in sample 4. The percentage of null subjects fluctuates until sample 7, and stabilizes thereafter.

The percentage of null subjects in Cheo's interlanguage is presented in Figure 4.2. As stated earlier, Cheo did not produce any English utterances during the first two sessions (samples 1 and 2), so, sample 3 represents Cheo's earliest attempts at producing English. In sample 3, Cheo omits subjects 20 % of the time, which is accounted for by only 2 instances out of a relatively small sample size of 10 utterances. The percentage of null subjects drops to 4.35% in the fourth sample and never goes above 10% in the subsequent samples.

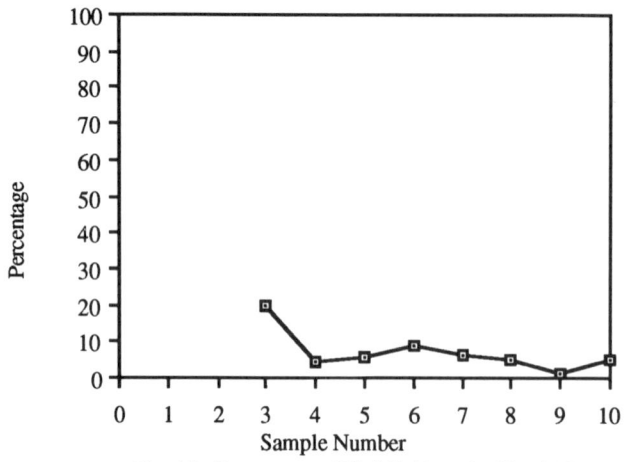

*Fig. 4.2: Percentage of Null Subjects in Cheo's IL*

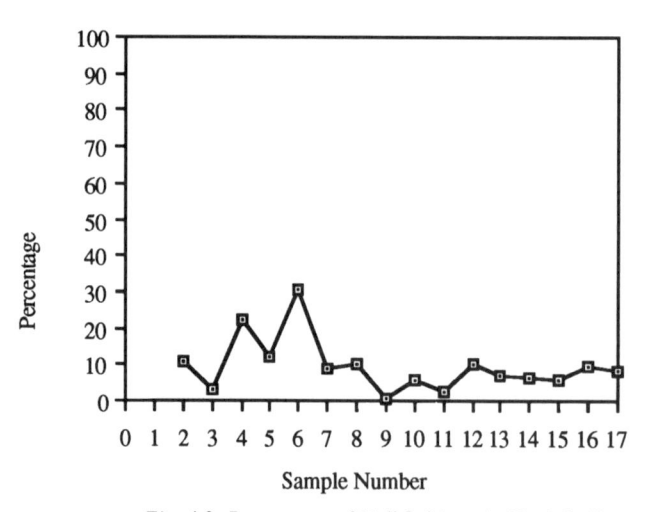

*Fig. 4.3: Percentage of Null Subjects in Muriel's IL*

The percentage of null subjects in Muriel's IL is displayed in Figure 4.3. In the case of Muriel, we see that the percentage of null subjects is quite low. Except for samples 3 to 6, the percentage of null subjects in the rest of the samples never goes above 10 %. When we compare the patterning of null subjects in

MORPHOLOGICAL UNIFORMITY AND NULL SUBJECTS 85

Muriel's IL with that of the two Spanish speaking subjects, we see that the percentage of null subjects fluctuates throughout.

Figure 4.4 shows the percentage of null subjects in Uguisu's IL. When we compare the percentage of null subjects in Uguisu's IL with that of the other

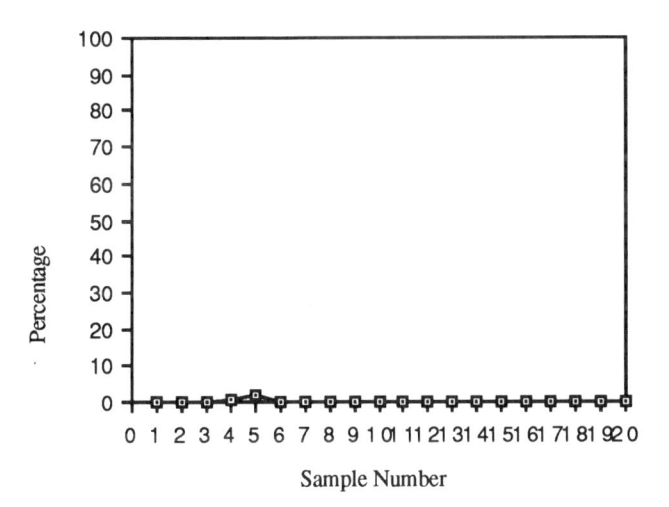

*Fig. 4.4: Percentage of Null Subjects in Uguisu's IL*

three subjects, we see that she hardly ever drops subjects. In all, there were only three instances of null subjects.[7] The first instance occurred in sample 4 and the other two instances occurred in sample 5. Even in the early samples, Uguisu produces utterances with expletive subjects as the examples in (5) indicate:

(5)     It's hot today        (sample 1)
        It's rain today       (Sample 3)

We stated earlier that although the results obtained for Uguisu were statistically significant they are not of practical significance. This is because Uguisu consistently retained subjects except for three instances. In other words, there is hardly any variation in Uguisu's use of subjectless utterances. The statistically significant results were probably obtained because all the three instances of null subjects occurred in the early consecutive samples. A comparison of the values for Fraction Explained by the Marginal model and the Fraction Explained by the

Full model also serves to support this conclusion. The Fraction explained by the Marginal model was found to be .9965 and the Fraction explained by the Full model was found to be .9970 . In other words, without taking into consideration the sample number (i.e. passage of time) we can account for 99% of Uguisu's IL with respect to null subjects. When we take time into account, our ability to predict only increases slightly (i.e. by .0005).

*4.3.1.2 Null Subjects versus Verb Inflections*

In order to verify the relationship between null subjects and verb inflections, least squares regression analyses (see Draper and Smith 1981) was done for each of the four subjects on the proportion of null subjects in each sample and the proportion of total inflections in each sample. The results of the least square regressions are shown in Table 4.4.

*Table 4.4: Results of Least Squares Regression on Null subjects and Inflections*

| Subject | Correlation Coefficient | Regression Coefficient | Significance |
|---------|------------------------|------------------------|--------------|
| Marta   | r = .26177             | $\beta$ = -.34816      | $p$ = .3460  |
| Cheo    | r = .85411             | $\beta$ = - .26188     | $p$ = .0069  |
| Muriel  | r = .32559             | $\beta$ = .37016       | $p$ = .2185  |
| Uguisu  | r = .59086             | $\beta$ = .43043 -1    | $p$ = .0061  |

The least squares regression analyses showed that there were two negative relations, for Marta and Cheo. Only the relation in Cheo's case was significant. There were two positive relations in the case of the other two subjects, Muriel and Uguisu. Of these, only the relation in the case of Uguisu was significant; however, as we explain below, the relation is not meaningful. Thus, only the IL of one subject provides evidence for the MUP.

Figure 4.5 shows the decrease in null subjects versus increase in inflections in Marta's IL There is considerable fluctuation in the percentage of inflections from sample 1 through 7. From sample 7 through 9, there is a dramatic increase in inflections by over 20 points, and from sample 9 through 15 the percentage of inflections never goes below 80%. When we examine the percentage of null subjects, we find that the dramatic decrease (over 40 points) in the percentage of null subjects occurs in sample 2. However, there is no corresponding dramatic increase in inflections in sample 2. What is interesting is that after some fluctuation, the percentage of null subjects gradually decreases from sample 7 onwards. This pattern may have contributed to the negative correlation that was observed with respect to this subject. As we saw above, the negative relation is not significant. Thus, Marta does not offer any evidence in support of the MUP.

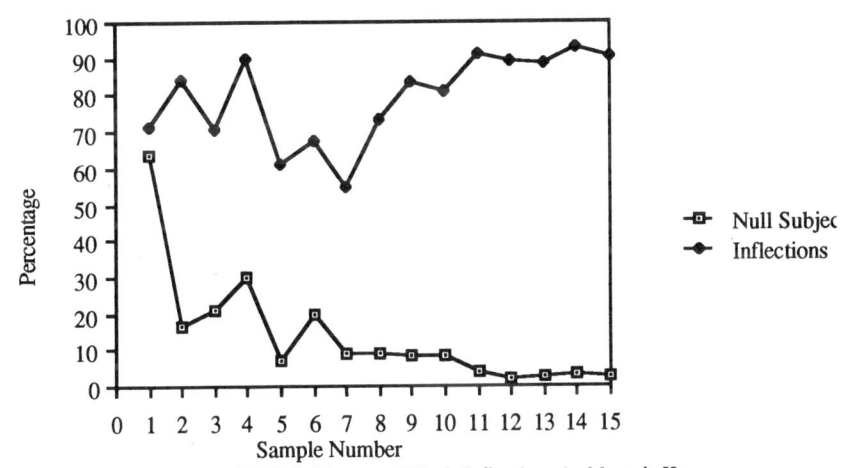

*Fig. 4.5: Percentage of Null Subjects and Verb Inflections in Marta's IL*

As we saw earlier, in Cheo's case, the least squares regression analysis provided evidence for the predictions of the MUP regarding the relations between null subjects and verb inflections. Figure 4.6 shows the decrease in null subjects versus increase in inflections.

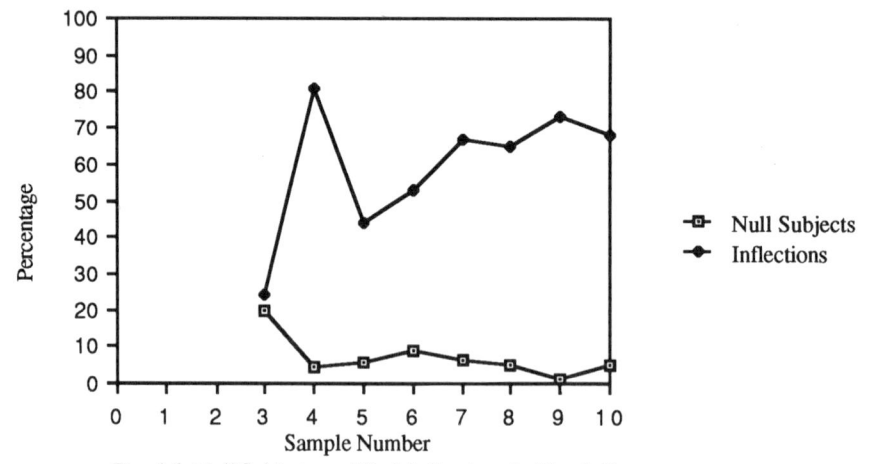

*Fig. 4.6: Null Subjects and Verb Inflections in Cheo's IL*

When we compare Cheo's IL with Marta's IL we find that he omits far more inflections than Marta in sample 3 where the percentage of inflections is around 24% (compare this figure with that of Marta's which is around 73%). In sample 4, the inflections increase to around 80%. Then, in sample 5, the inflections decrease to around 45%. Subsequently, the percentage of inflections steadily increases. However, it remains below 80% until the very last sample. In contrast, we find that (except in the case of sample 3) the percentage of null subjects never goes above 10%.

In terms of the predictions of the MUP, we would expect there to be a much higher percentage of null subjects in Cheo's IL, particularly in sample 3. But as the preceding discussion indicated, the percentage of null subjects in Cheo's IL is very low. This suggests that null subjects in Cheo's IL may at best be a weak effect of the MUP.

Fig 4.7 shows the incidence of null subjects versus the development of inflections in Muriel's IL. As we saw above, least squares regression showed that there is a positive relationship between development of inflections and omission of subjects. In other words, as inflections increase, null subjects also increase in Muriel's IL. However, the relation is not significant. Thus, as in the case of Marta's IL, Muriel's IL also does not offer any evidence in support of the MUP.

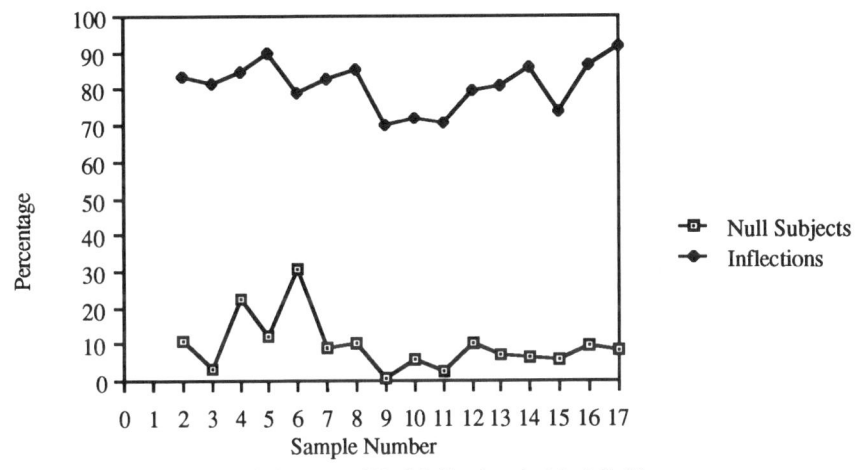

*Fig. 4.7: Null Subjects and Verb Inflections in Muriel's IL*

Figure 4.8 represents the percentage of null subjects versus inflection acquisition in Uguisu's IL.

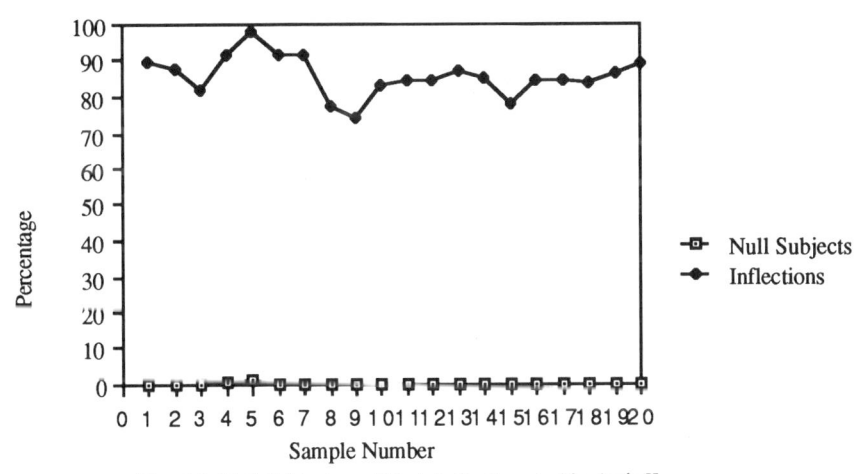

*Fig. 4.8: Null Subjects and Verb Inflections in Uguisu's IL*

As we saw above, the results of the regression analysis indicated a positive relation between inflections and null subjects in Uguisu's IL. Although the relation was shown to be significant, it is not meaningful. There are only three cases of null subjects and all of these occur in the earlier samples rather than the later ones. The significant effects were probably observed because of these early occurrences of null subjects. The $p$ value (see Table 4.3) indicates that a sizable proportion of the variation in the use of null subjects is explained by the proportion of inflections. However, β is close to zero, which indicates that there is not much variation in the occurrence of null subjects. In other words, it is not possible to predict the development of null subjects from the development of verb inflections. Again, as in the case of Muriel and Marta, Uguisu does not offer any evidence in support of the MUP.

*4.3.1.3 Relations between Inflection Acquisition and Type of Verb Morphology*

In examining the relationship between inflection acquisition and type of verb morphology, we did not carry out any statistical analyses to test for significance. Roger Brown in his study of the acquisition of English morphemes by first language learners (1973) devised a method for establishing criteria for acquisition of these morphemes. The linguistic feature must be present in 90% of all obligatory contexts in each transcript where five or more obligatory contexts exist, and the 90% criterion must be observed in three consecutive sessions. A similar method has been adopted in several longitudinal L2 studies as well (Hakuta 1973; Cazden, Cancino, Rosansky, Schumann, 1975; Gerbault 1978 among others). In order to identify the acquisition points for the different types of obligatory uses of inflections, we adopted a modified version of Brown's criterion. We considered the obligatory uses of inflection with respect to a particular morphological category as acquired in the first of three consecutive samples where the inflections are supplied 80% of the time, and where each sample consists of at least five obligatory uses.

The findings suggest that the obligatory uses of inflections are not learned at the same time but depend on the type of verb morphology. Table 4.5 below indicates the acquisition points for the obligatory uses of inflections for the different categories considered separately and considered together as one type (i.e. Total inflections). The dashes indicate that the subjects' uses of the inflection in question did not fulfill the 80% criterion. In addition, the point when subjects are supplied 80% of the time in three consecutive samples is also indicated. The third person irregular *does* (main verb) was not included as there were too few obligatory contexts for this inflection.

*Table 4.5: Acquisition points for the obligatory uses of inflections*

| Category | Marta | Cheo | Muriel | Uguisu |
|---|---|---|---|---|
| *Copula* | Sample 4 | Sample 6 | Sample 4 | Sample 1 |
| *Be (Aux)* | Sample 9 | --------- | Sample 7 | Sample 4 |
| *Do (Aux)* | --------- | --------- | Sample 5 | Sample 2 |
| *Have (Aux)* | --------- | --------- | --------- | --------- |
| *Modals* | Sample 9 | Sample 7 | Sample 9 | Sample 4 |
| *3rd sg regular* | --------- | --------- | --------- | --------- |
| *Past regular (ed)* | --------- | --------- | --------- | --------- |
| *Has (main verb)* | --------- | --------- | --------- | Sample 15 |
| *Total Inflections* | Sample 9 | --------- | Sample 2 | Sample 1 |
| *Subjects supplied* | Sample 5 | Sample 4 | Sample 7 | Sample 1 |

As we can see from Table 4.5, in the case of Marta, the obligatory uses of inflections are first acquired with respect to the copula (sample 4). Auxiliary *be* and modals are acquired at sample 9. Obligatory uses of inflections with respect to 3 rd person singular *-s* and the past regular *-ed* and *has* (main verb) and *do* aux are acquired beyond sample 15, as they never reach the criterion. When we compare the acquisition points of the various inflections with the percentage of null subjects, we do not observe a dramatic decrease in null subjects in sample 4, or 9. The dramatic decrease if anything appears earlier that is, in sample 2. However, as is evident from Table 4.5, the different types of inflections do not reach the 80% criterion by sample 2.

In the case of Cheo, none of the different types of verb morphology (with the exception of the copula and modals) satisfy the 80% criterion. The obligatory uses of inflections with respect to the copula satisfies the criterion in sample 6 and thereafter remains stable. As we saw earlier, around a 15 point decrease in null subjects occurs in sample 4, compared to only a slight decrease in null subjects from sample 6 through 8.

As in the case of Marta and Cheo, we see that the obligatory uses of inflections in Muriel's IL are not all learned at the same time but are acquired at different points. Inflections are first acquired with respect to the copula (sample 4). The following never reach the criterion: 3rd person singular *-s*, past *-ed*, *has* (main verb) and auxiliary *have*. Unlike Marta and Cheo, the obligatory uses of inflections with respect to auxiliary *do* is acquired by sample 5. When we examine the decrease in null subjects, we do not find a dramatic decrease in subjectless utterances beyond any of the acquisition points identified for the different types of inflections. In fact, null subjects never occur more than 10% of the time in all the samples with the exception of sample 6.

As in the case of the other three subjects, we notice that in the case of Uguisu, the different types of inflections are not acquired at the same time. Further, with the exception of *has* (main verb), inflections involving changes in the endings are never acquired at all.[8] However, what is interesting is that of the ones that are acquired (copula, auxiliaries *be, do,* modals*)*, all of them are acquired earlier by Uguisu when compared to the other subjects. Does this mean that Uguisu has realized that English is a [-uniform] language? There is some evidence that Uguisu does not assume that English is [ - uniform]. For example, as we will show in Chapter 5, there is evidence that Uguisu may consider English to be [+ uniform] (even in the last few samples). A similar tendency is also evidenced in the case of Muriel.

As we saw above, the predicted relationship between null subjects and verb inflections was supported only in Cheo's case but not with respect to the other three subjects, Marta, Muriel, and Uguisu. Of these three L2 learners, we saw that Uguisu did not treat English as a null subject language. She consistently supplied subjects throughout the time she was observed except for three instances which occurred during the early samples. On the other hand, Marta and Muriel appear to treat English as a null subject language. At the same time, we observed that like Cheo, Marta and Muriel, Uguisu initially omit inflections. We also found that the acquisition of verb inflections for all four subjects does not take place at once but appears to depend on the specific type of verb morphology. Even though Marta and Muriel failed to support the predictions of the MUP, we still need to explain their use of subjectless utterances. As we stated earlier, it is our hypothesis that *is* contexts play a major role in the occurrence of null subjects in these two learners' ILs. Let us now turn to the results of the analyses of the developmental and non-developmental relations between null subjects and *is* contexts.

### 4.3.2 *Relations between Null Subjects and 'Is-contexts'*

We stated in Chapter 3 that our preliminary study indicated that *is* contexts may be responsible for the occurrence of null subjects in these two learners' IL. For example, nearly all the null subjects in sample 1 in Marta's IL were found to occur in *is* (copula) contexts. Even in the subsequent samples, subject deletion occurred most frequently in *is* (copula and auxiliary) contexts. Although subject deletion also occurred in *non-is* contexts in the subsequent samples, there were fewer instances of these. The influence of *is* contexts is even more evident in the case of Muriel. In this subject's IL, all the instances of null subjects are in *is* contexts (except for two cases in sample 2). Further, the subject that is deleted in nearly all of such constructions is the referential/nonreferential *it*. Like Marta and Muriel, Cheo also deleted subjects from *is* constructions. However, a preliminary examination of each of Cheo's transcripts was not indicative of a strong association between *is* contexts and subject deletion. Subjects did not appear to be deleted more frequently in *is* contexts than in *non-is* contexts.

This section is organized as follows. First, we present the results with respect to the relationship between null subjects in *is* contexts and the development of *is* constructions. Next, we present the findings regarding the distribution of null subjects and lexically realized subjects in *is* and *non-is* contexts. The analysis of the relationship between null subjects and *is* contexts was not done for Uguisu since she hardly deleted subjects and further, none of the three instances of null subjects which occurred in her IL involved *is* contexts.

### 4.3.2.1 *Developmental Relations between Null Subjects and 'Is Constructions'*

In order to verify the relation between null subjects and *is* contexts, least squares regression was done on the proportion of null subjects in *is* contexts and the proportion of *is* contexts. Least squares regression was computed separately for three of the subjects, Marta, Cheo and Muriel.

Table 4.6 presents the results of the least squares regression analyses. The results of the least squares regressions showed a positive relation for only one subject (Marta) which was significant and two negative relations in the case of the other two subjects Muriel and Cheo. The two negative relations were not found to be significant.

*Table 4.6 : Results of Least Squares Regression on proportion of Null subjects in 'Is contexts' and proportion of 'Is contexts'*

| Subject | Correlation Coefficient | Regression Coefficient | Significance |
|---------|------------------------|------------------------|--------------|
| Marta   | r = .63098             | β = .43704             | p = .0117    |
| Cheo    | r = .12922             | β = -.23338            | p = .7604    |
| Muriel  | r = .01932             | β = - .38032 -1        | p = .9434    |

Figure 4.9 shows the development of null subjects in *is* constructions versus development of *is* constructions' in Marta's IL. Nearly all the null subjects in sample 1 were in *is* contexts. In order to verify whether the first sample was influencing the results, least squares regression was done without sample 1. However, the results still showed a positive relation between the development of null subjects in *is* contexts and the development of *is* constructions which was found to be significant (β= .20041; r = .54854; $p < .05$).

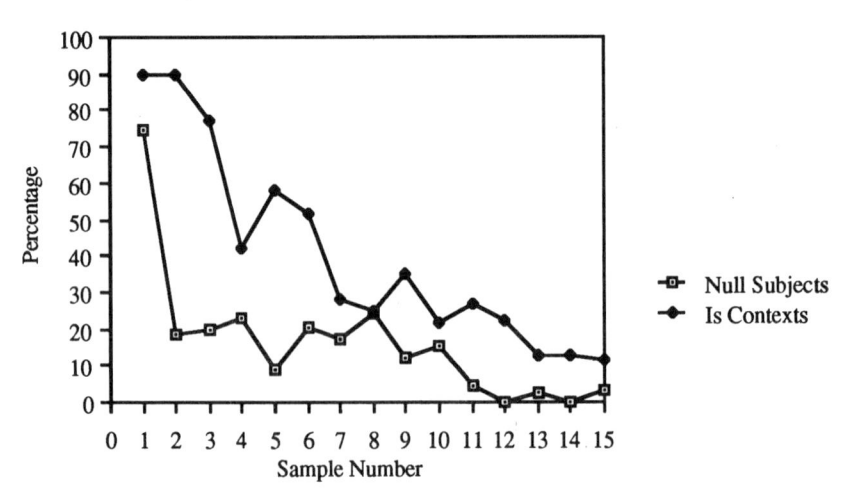

*Fig. 4.9: Null Subjects in 'Is Contexts' versus total 'Is Contexts' in Marta's IL*

# MORPHOLOGICAL UNIFORMITY AND NULL SUBJECTS

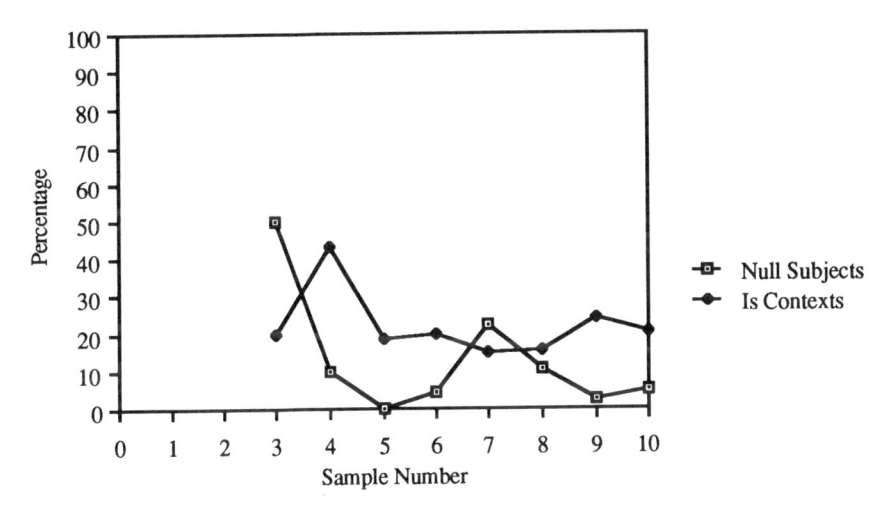

*Fig. 4.10: Null Subjects in 'Is Contexts' versus total 'Is Contexts' in Cheo's IL*

Fig. 4.10 presents the incidence of null subjects in *is* contexts versus development of *is* constructions in Cheo's IL. We stated earlier that in contrast with Marta, *is* contexts did not appear to be playing a role in the occurrence of null subjects in Cheo's IL. This is intriguing considering that both Cheo and Marta share the same L1; yet there is variation in their use of null subjects.

Fig. 4.11 shows the development of null subjects in *is* contexts versus development of *is* constructions in Muriel's IL. We stated earlier that the null subjects in Muriel's IL are restricted to *is* contexts. Yet, the regression analyses failed to show that increase in null subjects can be predicted by the increase in *is* contexts. It was felt that one of the reasons for these results might be related to the fact that in contrast with Marta, null subjects in the case of Muriel are not merely restricted to *is* contexts but more specifically to *is* contexts where the subject is referential or non referential *it*.

96  UNIVERSAL GRAMMAR IN CHILD SLA

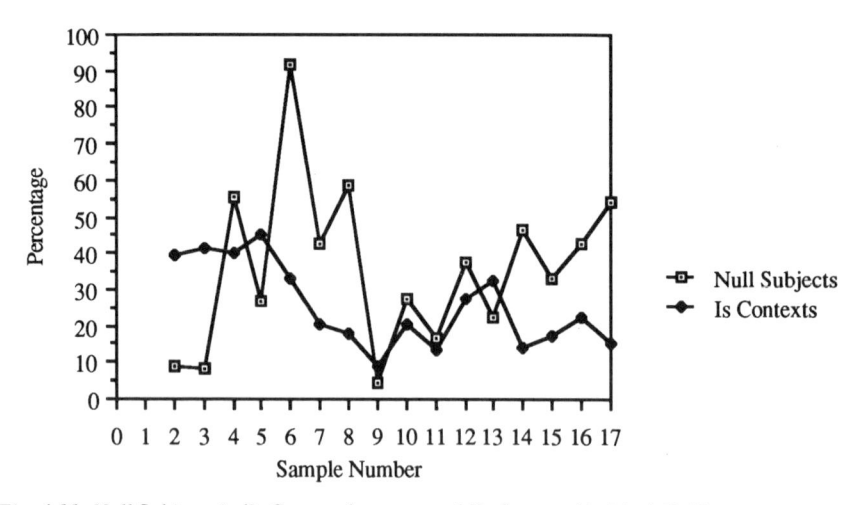

*Fig. 4.11: Null Subjects in 'Is Contexts' versus total 'Is Contexts' in Muriel's IL*

In order to verify whether the occurrence of null subjects and lexically realized subjects could be predicted from the context, namely *it is* contexts or *non-it is* contexts, null subjects and lexically realized subjects in *it is* contexts and *non-it is* contexts were separated. Logistic regression analyses were then carried out on the number of lexically realized subjects/null subjects and the number of *it is* and *non-it is* contexts. The results are presented in Table 4.7. Highly significant results were obtained ($p < .00001$) suggesting that subjects are more likely to be retained in a *non-it is* context and subjects are more likely to be deleted in an *it is* context. The values obtained for the Fraction explained by the Marginal model and Full model were .5191 and .7790 respectively. This indicates that when we take into account the context (i.e. whether it is an *it is* or an *non-it is* context), our ability to predict correctly increases by 25%.

*Table 4.7: Results of Logistic Regression on null subjects/ subjects in 'it is' contexts in Muriel's IL*

| Regression | Significance |
| --- | --- |
| β = 5.4196 | $p < .00001$ |

### 4.3.2.2. *Distribution of Null subjects/Subjects in 'is' and 'non-is' constructions*

Fishers exact probability[9] was carried out to test for significant differences between the distribution of null subjects/subjects in *is* contexts and *non-is* contexts. Fishers tests of exact probability were first done separately for each of the samples for three of the subjects, Marta, Cheo, and Uguisu. Next, the number of subjects and null subjects in *is* contexts and *non-is* contexts were summed over samples and Fishers exact was computed for the sum values thus obtained for these three subjects.

Only in the case of Marta and Muriel is there strong evidence that the differences between the occurrence of null subjects and subjects in *is* contexts' versus *non-is* contexts are not due to chance. There is also some evidence that *is* contexts may be playing a weak role in Cheo's case. The results of the Fishers test of exact probability for Marta, Cheo and Muriel are presented in Table 4.8, Table 4.9, and Table 4.10 respectively.

As can be seen from Table 4.8, in the case of Marta, significant results were obtained for sample 1, and samples 7 through 10. The results for sample 2 were close to being significant ($p < .06$). However, significant results were not obtained for samples 3 through 6 and samples 11 to 15. Significant results were also obtained when the occurrence of null-subjects and subjects were summed over samples ($p < 0.0000001$). What is interesting in Table 4.8 is the percentage of occurrences of null subjects in *is* contexts and *non-is* contexts. There is a decline in null subjects in *is* contexts from sample 1 to sample 4, while in the *non-is* contexts there is a steady increase. Sample 5 is small in size and therefore problematic but in sample 6 the percentage of the two types of occurrences are very close. After sample 7 the percentage of null subjects gradually tapers off and stabilizes thereafter. When we look at the figures for subjects supplied in *is* contexts, we can observe a sudden increase in subjects in sample 2. Nearly all of the utterances in these cases were of the *This is a* ___ type. From sample 7 onwards, there is an increase in the percentage of subjects in *non-is* contexts.

*Table 4.8: Results of Fishers Exact Probability: subjects and null subjects in Is and Non-is contexts in Marta's IL*

| Sample # | Is contexts |  |  |  | Non-is contexts |  |  |  | Significance |
|---|---|---|---|---|---|---|---|---|---|
|  | Null subjs |  | Subjs. |  | Null subjs. |  | Subjs. |  |  |
|  | n | % | n | % | n | % | n | % |  |
| S1 | 29 | 74.4 | 10 | 25.6 | 1 | 12.5 | 7 | 87.5 | $p$=.00193269 |
| S2 | 24 | 18.5 | 106 | 81.5 | 0 | 0.0 | 15 | 100.0 | $p$= .0567411 |
| S3 | 21 | 20.0 | 84 | 80.0 | 8 | 25.8 | 23 | 74.2 | $p$=.321239 |
| S4 | 16 | 23.9 | 51 | 76.1 | 32 | 34.8 | 60 | 65.2 | $p$= .0955852 |
| S5 | 3 | 9.1 | 30 | 90.9 | 1 | 4.2 | 23 | 95.8 | $p$= .435088 |
| S6 | 25 | 20.7 | 96 | 79.3 | 22 | 19.1 | 93 | 80.9 | $p$= .448170 |
| S7 | 18 | 17.3 | 86 | 82.7 | 16 | 6.1 | 248 | 93.9 | $p$= .00126430 |
| S8 | 12 | 24.0 | 38 | 76.0 | 6 | 4.0 | 145 | 96.0 | $p$=.000100050 |
| S9 | 16 | 12.2 | 115 | 87.8 | 14 | 5.8 | 228 | 94.2 | $p$=.0257542 |
| S10 | 11 | 15.3 | 61 | 84.7 | 16 | 6.2 | 242 | 93.8 | $p$=.0164131 |
| S11 | 4 | 4.4 | 87 | 95.6 | 8 | 3.2 | 239 | 96.8 | $p$=.411132 |
| S12 | 0 | 0.0 | 107 | 100 | 10 | 2.7 | 360 | 97.3 | $p$=.076011 |
| S13 | 2 | 2.6 | 75 | 97.4 | 13 | 2.5 | 501 | 97.5 | $p$=.603086 |
| S14 | 0 | 0.0 | 57 | 100 | 13 | 3.3 | 383 | 96.7 | $p$=.169738 |
| S15 | 2 | 3.4 | 56 | 96.6 | 12 | 2.7 | 429 | 97.3 | $p$= .498709 |
| Sum | 183 | 14.7 | 1059 | 85.3 | 172 | 5.4 | 2996 | 94.6 | $p$<.0000001 |

As can be seen from Table 4.9, in the case of Cheo, significant results were obtained only for sample 7 ($p$ < .00001). But when the samples were summed the differences between the distribution of subjects/null subjects in *is* and *non-is* contexts were found to be significant ($p$<.01). However, the level of significance is much lower when compared to what was obtained for Marta and Muriel (see Table 4.10). It is possible that the significant results obtained when the samples were summed may have been influenced by sample 7. As we can see from Table 4.9, null subjects rarely occur in *is* contexts in the early samples (sample 3-6). Then in sample 7 there is an increase in the number of null subjects in *is* contexts. In this connection it is interesting to note that verb inflections with respect to the *be* copula are acquired by sample 6. These facts suggest that *is* contexts may be playing a weak role with respect to null subjects in the later samples.

*Table 4.9: Results of Fishers Exact Tests: subjects and null subjects in Is and Non-is contexts in Cheo's IL*

| Sample # | Is contexts |  |  |  | Non-is contexts |  |  |  | Significance |
|---|---|---|---|---|---|---|---|---|---|
|  | Null subjs. |  | Subjs. |  | Null subjs. |  | Subjs. |  |  |
|  | n | % | n | % | n | % | n | % |  |
| S3 | 1 | 50.0 | 1 | 50.0 | 1 | 12.5 | 7 | 87.5 | $p = .377778$ |
| S4 | 1 | 10.0 | 9 | 90.0 | 0 | 0.0 | 13 | 100.0 | $p = .434783$ |
| S5 | 0 | 0.0 | 10 | 100 | 3 | 6.8 | 41 | 93.2 | $p = .533946$ |
| S6 | 2 | 4.2 | 46 | 95.8 | 19 | 9.6 | 178 | 90.4 | $p = .1788481$ |
| S7 | 13 | 22.4 | 45 | 77.6 | 12 | 3.6 | 325 | 96.4 | $p = .0000054$ |
| S8 | 5 | 10.4 | 43 | 89.6 | 10 | 3.9 | 248 | 96.1 | $p = .0675234$ |
| S9 | 2 | 2.2 | 87 | 97.8 | 3 | 1.1 | 275 | 98.9 | $p = .351295$ |
| S10 | 5 | 4.7 | 101 | 95.3 | 20 | 4.9 | 391 | 95.1 | $p = .592398$ |
| Sum | 29 | 7.8 | 342 | 92.2 | 68 | 4.4 | 1478 | 95.6 | $p = .00697259$ |

As Table 4.10 indicates, in the case of Muriel, except for samples 2, 3 and 9, the differences between the use/non-use of null subjects in *is* versus *non-is* contexts are highly significant for all the remaining samples. In addition, highly significant results were also obtained when the number of null subjects and subjects were summed across samples. When we compare Muriel's results with Marta's, we notice that significant differences are obtained even in the very last samples. This finding is strange considering that Muriel's first language is French, which is a non pro-drop language.

Table 4.10 : Results of Fishers Exact Tests: subjects and null subjects in 'is' and 'non-is' contexts in Muriel's IL

| Sample # | Is contexts Null subjs. n | Is contexts Null subjs. % | Is contexts Subjs. n | Is contexts Subjs. % | Non-is contexts Null subjs. n | Non-is contexts Null subjs. % | Non-is contexts Subjs. n | Non-is contexts Subjs. % | Significance |
|---|---|---|---|---|---|---|---|---|---|
| S2  | 1  | 9.1  | 10  | 90.9 | 2 | 11.8 | 15   | 88.2  | $p=.664225$ |
| S3  | 1  | 8.3  | 11  | 91.7 | 0 | 0.0  | 17   | 100.0 | $p=.413793$ |
| S4  | 20 | 55.6 | 16  | 44.4 | 0 | 0.0  | 54   | 100.0 | $p<.0000001$ |
| S5  | 10 | 27.0 | 27  | 73.0 | 0 | 0.0  | 45   | 100.0 | $p=.000162826$ |
| S6  | 22 | 91.7 | 2   | 8.3  | 0 | 0.0  | 48   | 100.0 | $p<.0000001$ |
| S7  | 12 | 42.9 | 16  | 57.1 | 0 | 0.0  | 109  | 100.0 | $p<.0000001$ |
| S8  | 21 | 58.3 | 15  | 41.7 | 0 | 0.0  | 168  | 100.0 | $p<.0000001$ |
| S9  | 1  | 4.3  | 22  | 95.7 | 0 | 0.0  | 234  | 100.0 | $p=.0894942$ |
| S10 | 17 | 27.4 | 45  | 72.6 | 0 | 0.0  | 237  | 100.0 | $p<.0000001$ |
| S11 | 7  | 16.7 | 35  | 83.3 | 0 | 0.0  | 267  | 100.0 | $p=.000000541$ |
| S12 | 24 | 37.5 | 40  | 62.5 | 0 | 0.0  | 167  | 100.0 | $p<.0000001$ |
| S13 | 25 | 22.5 | 86  | 77.5 | 0 | 0.0  | 230  | 100.0 | $p<.0000001$ |
| S14 | 15 | 46.9 | 17  | 53.1 | 0 | 0.0  | 194  | 100.0 | $p<.0000001$ |
| S15 | 7  | 33.3 | 14  | 66.7 | 0 | 0.0  | 103  | 100.0 | $p=.000001544$ |
| S16 | 12 | 42.9 | 16  | 57.1 | 0 | 0.0  | 97   | 100.0 | $p=.000000001$ |
| S17 | 35 | 53.8 | 30  | 46.2 | 0 | 0.0  | 357  | 100.0 | $p<.0000001$ |
| Sum | 230 | 36.4 | 402 | 63.6 | 2 | 0.1 | 2342 | 99.9 | $p<.0000001$ |

As we saw above, significant results were obtained for Cheo when Fishers exact was applied to the samples taken together. In order to verify the directionality of effects and measure the strength of the association between the predictor variable (i.e. *non-is* contexts and *is* contexts) and the predicted variables ( subjects supplied/null subjects) odds ratio analyses (see Fleiss 1981) was computed separately for the three subjects on the overall sample values. The formula used to compute the odds ratio was: $\dfrac{\dfrac{x}{y}}{\dfrac{w}{z}}$

(where x= Proportion of null subjects in *is* contexts, y = proportion of subjects supplied in *is* contexts, w= proportion of null subjects in *non-is* contexts, and z = proportion of subjects supplied in *non-is* contexts.)

An odds ratio of 1 would indicate that there is no directionality of effects. An odds ratio > 1 or < 1 would indicate that there is an association between the predictor variable and the predicted variable. If the odds ratio is > 1 then we can conclude that the predictor variable contributing to the strength of association is *is* contexts. If the odds ratio is obtained is < 1, then we would have to conclude that the *non-is* context is the predictor variable responsible for the effects. The odds ratio obtained for Cheo was 1.84. The odds ratio obtained for Marta was 3.01 and the odds ratio for Muriel was 670. These figures indicate that *is* contexts are responsible to varying degrees for these subjects' omission of subjects. The association between *is* contexts and null subjects is extremely strong with respect to Muriel. In the case of Marta, the association is also a strong one ( although considerably less so than in Muriel's case). The association between *is* contexts and null subjects in Cheo's IL is considerably weak compared to both Muriel and Marta. From the results of the analyses on the developmental and non-developmental relations between null subjects and *is* contexts it is evident that *is* contexts play a major role in Muriel's and Marta's use of subjectless utterances whereas its role with respect to Cheo's IL appears to be a weaker one. Null subjects in the IL of Marta and Muriel do not appear to be the result of parameter setting. As we will show in Chapter 5, the null subject phenomenon in the IL of these two learners appears to be the result of certain perceptual factors which specifically concern these subjects' perception and analysis of the unit *it's*.

## 4.4. Summary

The results reported in this chapter, do not offer any strong evidence in support of the predictions of the MUP. As we saw above, only one subject (Cheo) provides evidence for the MUP. In addition, we found evidence for the role of *is* contexts in the occurrence of null subjects, and we suggested that perceptual factors may be involved (at least with respect to Marta and Muriel). In our final chapter, we discuss in detail the implications of these findings for linguistic theory and for second language acquisition.

## Notes to Chapter 4

1. It is relevant to clarify that our use of the term "obligatory inflections" differs somewhat from its use in earlier SLA studies which were concerned with the acquisition of grammatical morphemes. In these studies, a particular grammatical morpheme was considered acquired if it was supplied in contexts where required and it lexically matched the form in the target language. As we will see in our discussion of the procedures adopted for the data analysis, the present study's concern was with whether overt coding for tense and/or agreement was present where it would be required in the target, regardless of whether the overt marking lexically matched the target form.

2. The last 10 transcripts of Uguisu's IL were examined for any variation in the use of null subjects and inflections. As in the previous samples, Uguisu consistently supplied subjects when required. At the same time, as in the previous samples, she continued to have problems with the obligatory use of inflections with respect to the Past regular *-ed* and 3rd person singular *-s*. Since the last 10 samples did not reveal any differences (at least with respect to Uguisu's use of verb inflections and subjects), they were not considered for the statistical analyses.

3. In Hakuta (1975), only a subset of the utterances (around 100) from each transcript formed the corpus of his study. However, for the purposes of the present research, each transcript was considered in its entirety.

4. Other examples of formulaic utterances which were not taken into account are *Whatsa matter, Buster?* in the case of Cheo and *I don't wanna* in the case of Uguisu.

5. Past irregular verbs such as *broke*, *went*, were not taken into account. It was felt that owing to their considerable lexical variation, each of the past irregular verbs would have to be learned one at a time (for a similar view, see Hakuta , 1975).

6. Instances of Verb + ing without an auxiliary, also occurred in a number of contexts including contexts where the progressive aspect would be unacceptable. As Schumann and others have stated, this use of Verb + ing is frequently observed in the speech of many Basilang speakers, and is usually analyzed as a variant of the base form of the verb. Such forms were also considered as uninflected forms.

7. In addition, Uguisu also omitted subjects from *It looks like a ----* constructions. Since such instances are acceptable in casual speech, they were not taken into account in the analysis. Some examples are given below:

> Look like an egg.
> Looks like an egg.
> Look like a baby.

8. As Hakuta (1976) has shown, the Past regular -*ed* morpheme and the present 3rd person singular are not acquired by Uguisu even by sample 30. As Hakuta has stated, one probable reason for this is that these morphemes are not salient as they involve changes in endings as opposed to changes in the root. For example, Hakuta found that Uguisu acquired *didn't* by sample 8, and *doesn't* and *did* by sample 17, both of which involve root changes.

9. It was necessary to carry out least squares regression analyses as well as Fishers tests of exact probability. The least squares regression analysis tested whether there was a relation between the development of null subjects in *is* constructions and the development of *is* constructions. This analysis therefore did not take into account the omission of subjects in *non-is* contexts. The Fishers test was intended to verify whether there were differences in the distribution of null subjects and the lexically realized subjects in *is* and *non-is* contexts.

## Appendix A

*Null subjects and inflections in Marta's IL*

| Sample | Null Subjects n | % | Verb Inflections n | % | Copula n | % |
|---|---|---|---|---|---|---|
| S1  | 30/47  | 63.8 | 35/49   | 71.4 | 32/40   | 80.0 |
| S2  | 24/145 | 16.6 | 126/150 | 84.0 | 121/136 | 89.0 |
| S3  | 29/136 | 21.3 | 98/138  | 71.0 | 95/122  | 77.8 |
| S4  | 48/159 | 30.2 | 73/81   | 90.1 | 57/59   | 96.6 |
| S5  | 4/57   | 7.0  | 36/59   | 61.0 | 31/36   | 86.1 |
| S6  | 47/236 | 19.9 | 127/189 | 67.2 | 96/104  | 92.3 |
| S7  | 34/368 | 9.2  | 128/235 | 54.5 | 89/100  | 89.0 |
| S8  | 18/201 | 8.9  | 79/108  | 73.1 | 43/45   | 95.6 |
| S9  | 30/373 | 8.0  | 226/271 | 83.4 | 107/155 | 93.0 |
| S10 | 27/330 | 8.2  | 155/192 | 80.7 | 40/47   | 85.1 |
| S11 | 12/338 | 3.6  | 259/285 | 90.9 | 89/93   | 95.7 |
| S12 | 10/477 | 2.1  | 268/300 | 89.3 | 107/111 | 96.4 |
| S13 | 15/591 | 2.5  | 347/393 | 88.3 | 111/114 | 97.4 |
| S14 | 13/453 | 2.9  | 247/265 | 93.2 | 52/55   | 94.5 |
| S15 | 14/499 | 2.8  | 245/271 | 90.4 | 61/69   | 88.4 |

*Null subjects and inflections in Marta's IL*

| Sample | Be (aux) n | Be (aux) % | Do (aux) n | Do (aux) % | Have (aux) n | Have (aux) % |
|---|---|---|---|---|---|---|
| S1 | 3/8 | 37.5 | ----- | ----- | 0/1 | 0.0 |
| S2 | 5/8 | 62.5 | 0/1 | 0.0 | ----- | ----- |
| S3 | 1/10 | 10.0 | 1/3 | 33.3 | ----- | ----- |
| S4 | 13/18 | 72.2 | ----- | ----- | ----- | ----- |
| S5 | 3/17 | 17.6 | ----- | ----- | ----- | ----- |
| S6 | 25/71 | 35.2 | 3/6 | 50.0 | 0/1 | 0.0 |
| S7 | 17/59 | 28.8 | 13/18 | 72.2 | 1/2 | 50.0 |
| S8 | 23/32 | 71.9 | 4/7 | 57.1 | ----- | ----- |
| S9 | 61/72 | 84.7 | 18/25 | 72.0 | 2/2 | 100.0 |
| S10 | 47/57 | 82.5 | 10/15 | 66.7 | ----- | ----- |
| S11 | 47/51 | 92.2 | 24/31 | 77.4 | 1/1 | 100.0 |
| S12 | 62/64 | 96.9 | 15/25 | 60.0 | 2/2 | 100.0 |
| S13 | 87/94 | 92.6 | 24/33 | 72.7 | ----- | ----- |
| S14 | 47/50 | 94.0 | 27/32 | 84.4 | 2/3 | 66.7 |
| S15 | 64/70 | 91.4 | 24/29 | 82.8 | 5/7 | 71.4 |

*Null subjects and inflections in Marta's IL*

| Sample | 3rd sg. regular n | % | Does (main verb) n | % | Has (main verb) n | % |
|---|---|---|---|---|---|---|
| S1  | ----- | ----- | ----- | ----- | ----- | ----- |
| S2  | 0/1   | 0.0   | ----- | ----- | ----- | ----- |
| S3  | ----- | ----- | ----- | ----- | ----- | ----- |
| S4  | 0/1   | 0.0   | ----- | ----- | 1/1   | 100.0 |
| S5  | 1/4   | 25.0  | 0/1   | 0.0   | ----- | ----- |
| S6  | 1/3   | 33.3  | ----- | ----- | ----- | ----- |
| S7  | 2/16  | 12.5  | 0/1   | 0.0   | 0/10  | 0.0   |
| S8  | 1/2   | 50.0  | 0/2   | 0.0   | 0/8   | 0.0   |
| S9  | 7/15  | 46.7  | 0/2   | 0.0   | 0/9   | 0.0   |
| S10 | 1/11  | 9.1   | ----- | ----- | 0/4   | 0.0   |
| S11 | 12/15 | 80.0  | ----- | ----- | 2/2   | 100.0 |
| S12 | 5/14  | 35.7  | ----- | ----- | 2/2   | 100.0 |
| S13 | 11/22 | 50.0  | ----- | ----- | 1/11  | 9.1   |
| S14 | 6/6   | 100.0 | ----- | ----- | 1/1   | 100.0 |
| S15 | 13/16 | 81.3  | ----- | ----- | ----- | ----- |

*Null subjects and inflections in Marta's IL*

| Sample | Past regular n | % | Modals n | % |
|---|---|---|---|---|
| S1 | ----- | ----- | ----- | ----- |
| S2 | 0/2 | 0.0 | 0/2 | 0.0 |
| S3 | 0/1 | 0.0 | 1/2 | 50.0 |
| S4 | ----- | ----- | 2/2 | 100.0 |
| S5 | ----- | ----- | 1/1 | 100.0 |
| S6 | 2/3 | 66.7 | 0/1 | 0.0 |
| S7 | 3/16 | 18.8 | 3/13 | 23.1 |
| S8 | 0/1 | 0.0 | 8/11 | 72.7 |
| S9 | 1/1 | 100.0 | 30/30 | 100.0 |
| S10 | 1/1 | 100.0 | 56/57 | 98.2 |
| S11 | 6/10 | 60.0 | 78/82 | 95.1 |
| S12 | 7/14 | 50.0 | 68/68 | 100.0 |
| S13 | 7/13 | 53.8 | 106/106 | 100.0 |
| S14 | 10/15 | 66.7 | 102/103 | 99.0 |
| S15 | 6/6 | 100.0 | 72/74 | 97.3 |

## Appendix B

*Null subjects and inflections in Cheo's IL*

| Sample | Null Subjects n | % | Verb Inflections n | % | Copula n | % |
|---|---|---|---|---|---|---|
| S3 | 2/10 | 20.0 | 6/25 | 24.0 | 5/20 | 25.0 |
| S4 | 1/23 | 4.3 | 17/21 | 80.9 | 11/13 | 84.6 |
| S5 | 3/54 | 5.5 | 14/32 | 43.8 | 8/11 | 72.7 |
| S6 | 21/245 | 8.6 | 70/133 | 52.6 | 40/45 | 88.9 |
| S7 | 25/395 | 6.3 | 143/213 | 67.1 | 55/59 | 93.2 |
| S8 | 15/306 | 4.9 | 116/179 | 64.8 | 49/58 | 84.5 |
| S9 | 5/367 | 1.4 | 172/235 | 73.2 | 67/70 | 95.7 |
| S10 | 25/517 | 4.8 | 214/315 | 67.9 | 118/129 | 91.5 |

*Null subjects and inflections in Cheo's IL*

| Sample | Be (aux) n | % | Do (aux) n | % | Have (aux) n | % |
|---|---|---|---|---|---|---|
| S3 | ----- | ----- | 0/4 | 0.0 | ----- | ----- |
| S4 | 1/1 | 100.0 | 4/4 | 100.0 | ----- | ----- |
| S5 | 1/4 | 25.0 | 1/10 | 10.0 | ----- | ----- |
| S6 | 6/11 | 54.5 | 12/32 | 37.5 | 1/5 | 20.0 |
| S7 | 19/33 | 57.6 | 24/44 | 54.5 | 2/2 | 100.0 |
| S8 | 22/33 | 66.7 | 4/16 | 25.0 | 2/7 | 28.6 |
| S9 | 40/75 | 53.3 | 17/25 | 68.0 | 0/3 | 0.0 |
| S10 | 16/25 | 64.0 | 21/36 | 58.3 | 6/36 | 16.7 |

*Null subjects and inflections in Cheo's IL*

| Sample | 3rd sg. regular n | % | Does (main verb) n | % | Has (main verb) n | % |
|---|---|---|---|---|---|---|
| S3 | ----- | ----- | ----- | ----- | ----- | ----- |
| S4 | 1/3 | 33.3 | ----- | ----- | ----- | ----- |
| S5 | 1/3 | 33.3 | ----- | ----- | ----- | ----- |
| S6 | 2/20 | 10.0 | ----- | ----- | 0/1 | 0.0 |
| S7 | 3/20 | 15.0 | ----- | ----- | 1/16 | 6.3 |
| S8 | 4/17 | 23.5 | ----- | ----- | 0/5 | 0.0 |
| S9 | 1/10 | 10.0 | ----- | ----- | 0/2 | 0.0 |
| S10 | 9/33 | 27.3 | ----- | ----- | 1/6 | 16.7 |

*Null subjects and inflections in Cheo's IL*

| Sample | Past regular n | % | Modals n | % |
|---|---|---|---|---|
| S3 | ----- | ----- | 1/1 | 100.0 |
| S4 | ----- | ----- | ----- | ----- |
| S5 | 0/1 | 0.0 | 3/3 | 100.0 |
| S6 | 2/2 | 100.0 | 7/17 | 41.2 |
| S7 | 1/1 | 100.0 | 38/38 | 100.0 |
| S8 | 2/4 | 50.0 | 33/39 | 84.6 |
| S9 | 3/5 | 60.0 | 44/45 | 97.8 |
| S10 | 1/6 | 16.7 | 42/44 | 95.5 |

## Appendix C

*Null subjects and inflections in Muriel's IL*

| Sample | Null Subjects n | % | Verb Inflections n | % | Copula n | % |
|---|---|---|---|---|---|---|
| S2  | 3/28    | 10.7 | 15/18   | 83.3 | 11/12 | 91.7 |
| S3  | 1/29    | 3.4  | 26/32   | 81.3 | 15/20 | 75.0 |
| S4  | 20/90   | 22.2 | 50/59   | 84.7 | 25/29 | 86.2 |
| S5  | 10/82   | 12.2 | 53/59   | 89.8 | 28/30 | 93.3 |
| S6  | 22/72   | 30.6 | 38/48   | 79.2 | 21/25 | 84.0 |
| S7  | 12/137  | 8.8  | 71/86   | 82.6 | 24/26 | 92.3 |
| S8  | 21/204  | 10.3 | 169/198 | 85.4 | 38/46 | 82.6 |
| S9  | 1/257   | 0.4  | 64/91   | 70.3 | 30/34 | 88.2 |
| S10 | 17/299  | 5.7  | 158/220 | 71.8 | 70/83 | 84.3 |
| S11 | 7/309   | 2.3  | 134/189 | 70.9 | 41/44 | 93.2 |
| S12 | 24/231  | 10.4 | 140/176 | 79.5 | 70/84 | 83.3 |
| S13 | 25/341  | 7.3  | 160/197 | 81.2 | 75/76 | 98.7 |
| S14 | 15/226  | 6.6  | 120/139 | 86.3 | 49/50 | 98.0 |
| S15 | 7/124   | 5.6  | 49/66   | 74.2 | 16/18 | 88.9 |
| S16 | 12/125  | 9.6  | 71/82   | 86.6 | 17/19 | 89.5 |
| S17 | 35/422  | 8.3  | 242/264 | 91.7 | 90/92 | 97.8 |

*Null subjects and inflections in Muriel's IL*

| Sample | Be (aux) n | Be (aux) % | Do (aux) n | Do (aux) % | Have (aux) n | Have (aux) % |
|---|---|---|---|---|---|---|
| S2  | 0/2   | 0.0   | 1/1   | 100.0 | 1/1   | 100.0 |
| S3  | ----- | ----- | 8/9   | 88.9  | ----- | ----- |
| S4  | 17/18 | 94.4  | 1/1   | 100.0 | 4/4   | 100.0 |
| S5  | 4/4   | 100.0 | 15/18 | 83.3  | ----- | ----- |
| S6  | 6/9   | 66.7  | 4/4   | 100.0 | ----- | ----- |
| S7  | 23/25 | 92.0  | 14/16 | 87.5  | 3/3   | 100.0 |
| S8  | 66/73 | 90.4  | 36/36 | 100.0 | 7/7   | 100.0 |
| S9  | 12/12 | 100.0 | 10/10 | 100.0 | ----- | ----- |
| S10 | 17/27 | 63.0  | 4/7   | 57.1  | 1/10  | 10.0  |
| S11 | 25/48 | 52.1  | 13/15 | 86.7  | 13/22 | 59.1  |
| S12 | 32/34 | 94.1  | 21/24 | 87.5  | 0/8   | 0.0   |
| S13 | 46/55 | 83.6  | 14/24 | 58.3  | 3/3   | 100.0 |
| S14 | 9/14  | 64.3  | 27/27 | 100.0 | 2/2   | 100.0 |
| S15 | 5/6   | 83.3  | 11/21 | 52.4  | ----- | ----- |
| S16 | 14/18 | 77.8  | 32/34 | 94.1  | ----- | ----- |
| S17 | 29/33 | 87.9  | 40/42 | 95.2  | 1/3   | 33.33 |

*Null subjects and inflections in Muriel's IL*

| Sample | 3rd sg. regular n | % | Does (main verb) n | % | Has (main verb) n | % |
|---|---|---|---|---|---|---|
| S2  | ----- | ----- | ----- | ----- | ----- | ----- |
| S3  | ----- | ----- | 1/1 | 100.0 | ----- | ----- |
| S4  | 0/4 | 0.0 | ----- | ----- | ----- | ----- |
| S5  | ----- | ----- | ----- | ----- | 0/1 | 0.0 |
| S6  | 1/1 | 100.0 | ----- | ----- | ----- | ----- |
| S7  | 1/3 | 33.3 | ----- | ----- | ----- | ----- |
| S8  | 3/4 | 75.0 | ----- | ----- | 0/2 | 0.0 |
| S9  | 1/3 | 33.3 | ----- | ----- | ----- | ----- |
| S10 | 0/4 | 0.0 | ----- | ----- | ----- | ----- |
| S11 | 1/4 | 25.0 | ----- | ----- | ----- | ----- |
| S12 | 2/3 | 66.7 | ----- | ----- | ----- | ----- |
| S13 | 1/2 | 50.0 | ----- | ----- | 2/16 | 12.50 |
| S14 | 0/9 | 0.0 | 0/1 | 0.0 | 0/1 | 0.0 |
| S15 | 1/1 | 100.0 | ----- | ----- | 0/1 | 0.0 |
| S16 | 3/4 | 75.0 | ----- | ----- | ----- | ----- |
| S17 | 8/12 | 66.7 | ----- | ----- | ----- | ----- |

*Null subjects and inflections in Muriel's IL*

| Sample | Past regular n | % | Modals n | % |
|---|---|---|---|---|
| S2  | ----- | ----- | 2/2   | 100.0 |
| S3  | ----- | ----- | 2/2   | 100.0 |
| S4  | 3/3   | 100.0 | ----- | ----- |
| S5  | ----- | ----- | 6/6   | 100.0 |
| S6  | ----- | ----- | 6/9   | 66.7  |
| S7  | 0/1   | 0.0   | 6/12  | 50.0  |
| S8  | 4/4   | 100.0 | 15/26 | 57.7  |
| S9  | 6/27  | 22.2  | 5/5   | 100.0 |
| S10 | 4/22  | 18.2  | 62/67 | 92.5  |
| S11 | 3/11  | 27.3  | 38/45 | 84.4  |
| S12 | 0/4   | 0.0   | 15/19 | 78.9  |
| S13 | ----- | ----- | 19/21 | 90.5  |
| S14 | 2/4   | 50.0  | 31/31 | 100.0 |
| S15 | 1/1   | 100.0 | 15/18 | 83.3  |
| S16 | 1/2   | 50.0  | 4/5   | 80.0  |
| S17 | 2/8   | 25.0  | 72/74 | 97.3  |

## Appendix D

*Null subjects and inflections in Uguisu's IL*

| Sample | Null Subjects n | % | Verb Inflections n | % | Copula n | % |
|---|---|---|---|---|---|---|
| S1 | 0/102 | 0.0 | 87/97 | 89.6 | 66/72 | 91.7 |
| S2 | 0/179 | 0.0 | 150/171 | 87.7 | 104/120 | 86.7 |
| S3 | 0/220 | 0.0 | 158/193 | 81.9 | 94/106 | 88.7 |
| S4 | 1/114 | 0.9 | 88/96 | 91.7 | 40/43 | 93.0 |
| S5 | 2/122 | 1.6 | 102/104 | 98.1 | 51/52 | 98.1 |
| S6 | 0/233 | 0.0 | 202/220 | 91.8 | 49/59 | 83.1 |
| S7 | 0/123 | 0.0 | 89/97 | 91.7 | 41/43 | 95.3 |
| S8 | 0/382 | 0.0 | 181/234 | 77.4 | 69/86 | 80.2 |
| S9 | 0/450 | 0.0 | 234/315 | 74.3 | 126/147 | 85.7 |
| S10 | 0/615 | 0.0 | 323/389 | 83.0 | 136/146 | 93.2 |
| S11 | 0/466 | 0.0 | 219/259 | 84.6 | 107/113 | 94.7 |
| S12 | 0/561 | 0.0 | 326/386 | 84.5 | 151/157 | 96.2 |
| S13 | 0/582 | 0.0 | 276/316 | 87.3 | 142/149 | 95.3 |
| S14 | 0/427 | 0.0 | 247/291 | 84.9 | 140/149 | 94.0 |
| S15 | 0/343 | 0.0 | 179/230 | 77.8 | 109/112 | 97.3 |
| S16 | 0/558 | 0.0 | 325/385 | 84.4 | 170/173 | 98.3 |
| S17 | 0/344 | 0.0 | 196/232 | 84.5 | 98/102 | 96.1 |
| S18 | 0/641 | 0.0 | 308/368 | 83.7 | 137/139 | 98.6 |
| S19 | 0/549 | 0.0 | 288/333 | 86.5 | 146/152 | 96.1 |
| S20 | 0/592 | 0.0 | 284/319 | 89.0 | 121/135 | 89.6 |

*Null subjects and inflections in Uguisu's IL*

| Sample | Be (aux) n | % | Do (aux) n | % | Have (aux) n | % |
|---|---|---|---|---|---|---|
| S1  | 14/15 | 93.3  | 4/4   | 100.0 | ----- | ----- |
| S2  | 32/34 | 94.1  | 12/13 | 92.3  | ----- | ----- |
| S3  | 48/66 | 72.7  | 10/11 | 90.9  | ----- | ----- |
| S4  | 21/23 | 91.3  | 16/17 | 94.1  | ----- | ----- |
| S5  | 18/19 | 94.7  | 23/23 | 100.0 | ----- | ----- |
| S6  | 38/41 | 92.7  | 44/49 | 89.8  | ----- | ----- |
| S7  | 7/7   | 100.0 | 23/23 | 100.0 | ----- | ----- |
| S8  | 16/23 | 69.6  | 43/54 | 79.6  | ----- | ----- |
| S9  | 24/48 | 50.0  | 33/45 | 73.3  | ----- | ----- |
| S10 | 20/36 | 55.6  | 48/59 | 81.4  | 0/3   | 0.0   |
| S11 | 21/30 | 70.0  | 26/38 | 68.4  | 0/1   | 0.0   |
| S12 | 40/67 | 59.7  | 57/62 | 91.9  | 0/3   | 0.0   |
| S13 | 30/43 | 69.8  | 24/26 | 92.3  | 1/10  | 10.0  |
| S14 | 29/50 | 58.0  | 30/31 | 96.8  | 2/4   | 50.0  |
| S15 | 20/56 | 35.7  | 14/17 | 82.4  | 2/3   | 66.7  |
| S16 | 40/77 | 51.9  | 22/26 | 84.6  | 5/5   | 100.0 |
| S17 | 34/61 | 55.7  | 14/15 | 93.3  | 2/2   | 100.0 |
| S18 | 56/85 | 65.9  | 28/30 | 93.3  | 1/1   | 100.0 |
| S19 | 37/62 | 59.7  | 30/32 | 93.8  | 3/3   | 100.0 |
| S20 | 52/61 | 85.2  | 26/26 | 100.0 | 17/18 | 94.4  |

*Null subjects and inflections in Uguisu's IL*

| Sample | 3rd sg. regular n | % | Does (main verb) n | % | Has (main verb) n | % |
|---|---|---|---|---|---|---|
| S1  | 0/3   | 0.0   | ----- | ----- | ----- | ----- |
| S2  | 2/2   | 100.0 | ----- | ----- | ----- | ----- |
| S3  | 2/6   | 33.3  | ----- | ----- | ----- | ----- |
| S4  | 1/3   | 33.3  | ----- | ----- | ----- | ----- |
| S5  | ----- | ----- | ----- | ----- | ----- | ----- |
| S6  | 9/9   | 100.0 | ----- | ----- | 1/1   | 100.0 |
| S7  | 1/2   | 50.0  | ----- | ----- | 0/1   | 0.0   |
| S8  | 10/15 | 66.7  | ----- | ----- | 5/5   | 100.0 |
| S9  | 2/14  | 14.3  | ----- | ----- | 1/1   | 100.0 |
| S10 | 6/21  | 28.6  | ----- | ----- | 4/6   | 66.7  |
| S11 | 4/12  | 33.3  | ----- | ----- | 1/1   | 100.0 |
| S12 | 1/6   | 16.7  | ----- | ----- | 2/2   | 100.0 |
| S13 | 9/13  | 69.2  | ----- | ----- | ----- | ----- |
| S14 | 2/7   | 28.6  | ----- | ----- | 0/1   | 0.0   |
| S15 | 7/9   | 77.8  | ----- | ----- | 4/4   | 100.0 |
| S16 | 9/20  | 45.0  | ----- | ----- | 12/12 | 100.0 |
| S17 | 8/11  | 72.7  | ----- | ----- | ----- | ----- |
| S18 | 16/29 | 55.1  | ----- | ----- | 12/12 | 100.0 |
| S19 | ----- | ----- | ----- | ----- | ----- | ----- |
| S20 | 16/21 | 76.2  | 0/1   | 0.0   | 4/4   | 100.0 |

*Null subjects and inflections in Uguisu's IL*

| Sample | Past regular n | % | Modals n | % |
|---|---|---|---|---|
| S1 | 2/2 | 100.0 | 1/1 | 100.0 |
| S2 | 0/2 | 0.0 | ----- | ----- |
| S3 | ----- | ----- | 4/4 | 100.0 |
| S4 | ----- | ----- | 10/10 | 100.0 |
| S5 | ----- | ----- | 10/10 | 100.0 |
| S6 | 2/2 | 100.0 | 59/59 | 100.0 |
| S7 | 0/2 | 0.0 | 17/19 | 89.5 |
| S8 | 6/18 | 33.3 | 32/33 | 97.0 |
| S9 | 7/17 | 41.2 | 41/43 | 95.3 |
| S10 | 4/11 | 36.4 | 105/107 | 98.1 |
| S11 | 1/4 | 25.0 | 59/60 | 98.3 |
| S12 | 4/17 | 23.5 | 71/72 | 98.6 |
| S13 | 5/10 | 50.0 | 65/65 | 100.0 |
| S14 | 10/15 | 66.7 | 34/34 | 100.0 |
| S15 | 1/7 | 14.3 | 22/22 | 100.0 |
| S16 | 5/8 | 62.5 | 62/64 | 96.9 |
| S17 | 6/7 | 85.7 | 34/34 | 100.0 |
| S18 | 3/11 | 27.3 | 55/61 | 90.2 |
| S19 | 5/12 | 41.7 | 67/72 | 93.1 |
| S20 | 5/9 | 55.6 | 43/44 | 97.7 |

# 5 Discussion and Conclusions

## 5.0. An Overview

In the previous chapter we presented the results of the study in terms of the research questions addressed. The following is a summary of the main findings with respect to the IL development of the four subjects: Marta, Cheo, Muriel and Uguisu.

I. Relations between Verb inflections and Null subjects:

(a) For all four subjects, statistically significant results were obtained for a developmental relation between null subjects and passage of time suggesting that null subjects in these learners' ILs occurred more often in the earlier rather than in the later samples. However, since Uguisu, the native speaker of Japanese, consistently retained subjects except for three instances in the early samples, the results with respect to this subject were not found to be of practical significance.

(b) Only one subject (Cheo) gave evidence for the relation predicted by the MUP between the development of verb inflections and the use of null subjects.

(c) For all four subjects, it was found that the obligatory uses of inflections are not acquired all at once; instead, the evidence suggests that acquisition of these inflections depends on the specific type of verb morphology.

II. Relations between null-subjects and *is* contexts:

(a) One subject (Marta) provided evidence for the developmental relation between null subjects in *is* constructions and *is* constructions. The proportion of null subjects in *is* constructions was found to increase with the increase in the proportion of *is* constructions. While similar findings were not obtained for

Muriel, a finer analysis revealed that the *it is* context is a strong predictor of the occurrence of null subjects in this subject's IL.

(b) Significant differences in the distribution of null subjects and lexically realized subjects in *is* contexts and *non-is* contexts was found for Marta and Muriel (7 out of 15 samples for Marta and 14 out of 17 samples for Muriel). Significant results were also obtained for these two subjects when the samples for each subject were considered together. Thus, the findings gave strong evidence of a non-developmental relation between null subjects and *is* contexts. In addition, Cheo also provided some evidence of a non-developmental relation between *is* contexts and null subjects. However, in Cheo's case statistically significant differences in the distribution of null subjects and lexically realized subjects in *is* contexts and *non-is* contexts were found only with respect to one sample (sample 7) and when summing over samples was done (this, as stated earlier, was probably due to sample 7).

(c) The results of the odds ratio analyses indicated a strong association between *is* contexts and null subjects for Muriel and Marta (the association in the former being by far the strongest). In Cheo's case, the association between *is* contexts and null subjects was considerably weaker compared to the other two subjects. The findings of the odds ratio analyses thus suggest that *is* contexts play a major role in Marta's and Muriel's IL and a possibly weak one in Cheo's case.

In the following sections we discuss the implications of the above findings and present our conclusions.

## 5.1. Discussion

This section is organized as follows. First, we discuss the implications of our findings for the theoretical construct of the MUP, which is intended to account for the null subject phenomenon in adult and child grammars. Next, we discuss the role of perceptual factors and the L1 in the IL development of the four subjects, Marta, Cheo, Muriel and Uguisu. Third, we outline some of the possible reasons for the observed individual differences. Fourth, we discuss the implications of our findings for a UG based theory of SLA.

## 5.1.1. Implications of the Findings for the MUP

Overall, the findings of this study do not offer strong evidence for the MUP or of child L2 learners' accessibility to this principle. Of the four subjects, only Cheo's IL provides evidence for the predictions of the MUP. In what follows we examine some of the problems that our data pose for the theoretical construct of the MUP.

The first problem concerns the predictions of the MUP regarding the relationship between verb inflections and null subjects. The MUP predicts that when inflections emerge in the developing grammar of a language that is [-uniform], null subjects should be abandoned. In other words, we would not expect to find null subjects occurring with inflected verbs. As we saw in Chapter 3, data from the early grammars of French (Weissenborn 1992) and child initiated revisions in the early grammars of English (Shatz and Ebeling 1991) provide evidence that null-subjects do not disappear abruptly or entirely when verb inflections are acquired.

Weissenborn's and Shatz and Ebeling's findings are also supported by the data from Marta's and Cheo's ILs. An examination of the transcripts of these two subjects revealed the presence of utterances where verb inflections are supplied but subjects are still deleted. This is illustrated by the examples in (1). The examples in (1a) are from Marta and the examples in (1b) are from Cheo.

1a. Goes right in the street. (Sample 5)
Are flowers? (Sample 6)
Speaks English and Spanish. (sample 9)
Bites me here. (Sample 9)
Says don't walk. (sample 9)
Only was my father. (sample 11)

1b. Why they came xxx and he's not home and he came and (haves) something with/ where his mouth? (sample 10)
And are stronger too. (sample 10)
Why don't need anybody get here? (sample 10)

Thus, the evidence suggests that a change from a stage where subjects are optionally overt to a stage where subjects are not omitted is a gradual one and may not be the result of parameter setting.

# DISCUSSION AND CONCLUSIONS

Data from Uguisu and Muriel also pose problems for the predicted relationship between the [+ uniform] setting of the MUP and null-subjects. In the case of Uguisu, we observed that she initially omits inflections. We also noticed that inflections involving changes in the endings never reach the 80% criterion. Yet null subjects are a rarity in Uguisu's IL. Further, there is evidence that when the present third person singular (regular and irregular) emerges, the overt marking is incorrectly extended to other subject pronouns. This is illustrated by the following examples in (2) [1]:

 2. The children doesn't eat.
    We both has.
    If the people comes.
    My feet hurts.
    You just wants.
    Here I goes the orange.
    People goes...
    I wants to..
    My father and mother doesn't cry.
    Here we goes.
    You likes me.

Muriel also uses a similar strategy which is illustrated by the utterances in (3).

 3. I knows a lot.
    you haves.
    I haves...

Hyams and Jaeggli are silent about the possibility of such occurrences. In their view the emergence of past and present inflections is an indication that the child has correctly realized that English is a [- uniform] language. What such a proposal does not explain is the incorrect generalization of these inflections to other persons. In other words, from the above data it is not clear that Uguisu and Muriel have indeed correctly assumed that English is [- uniform]. On the other hand, their over generalizations may be seen as an attempt to make the verb paradigms in their grammar [+ uniform]. In terms of the MUP we would expect to see subjects deleted from such utterances. In both Uguisu's and Muriel's IL, the extension of the third person singular marking to other persons occurs in the later samples. In Uguisu's case subjectless utterances never occur. In Muriel's case, although subjectless utterances occur, they are restricted to *is* contexts and subjects are never dropped from utterances as in (3) above.

A second problem concerns Hyams' and Jaeggli's claims that the subset principle would account for the learnability problem with respect to verb inflections. As we saw earlier, Hyams and Jaeggli argue that [+ uniform] is the initial/default setting. In terms of the subset principle, a [+ uniform] language is a smaller language than a [- uniform] language. Hence, in their analyses, if [- uniform] were the default setting, then children learning a [+ uniform] language would not be able to shift to a [+ uniform] stage as they would not encounter positive evidence that the language is [+ uniform]. We saw in Chapter 3 that the early grammars of richly inflected null subject languages cannot be adequately captured by the subset principle. Specifically, with respect to the early grammars of Italian, we demonstrated that there could be a [ - uniform] stage mediating the [+ uniform] [- inflected] stage and the [+ uniform] [+ inflected] stage. However, the subset principle predicts that the child can never move out from a larger grammar [ - uniform] to a smaller grammar [+ uniform + inflected]. As we saw above, the generalizations that Uguisu and Muriel make with respect to the present third person singular (regular and irregular) provide evidence that this is indeed possible. Thus, the subset principle fails to solve the learnability problem, at least with respect to the notion of morphological uniformity.

Another problem for the claim that [+ uniform] is the default setting is posed by the use of the copula *is*. Several studies have shown that the copula appears relatively early in L2 learners' speech (Cancino, Rosansky and Schumann 1974; Dulay and Burt 1974; Hakuta 1975; Felix 1976; Nicholas 1981; Tiphine 1983). Data from Muriel and Marta suggest that *is* is not only used as a copula but also occurs instead of a lexical (thematic) verb, as the examples in (4) illustrate.

4. King is an apple
[ King wants an apple]                (Muriel,Sample 3)
Christine is the class.
[Christine teaches the class]          (Marta, Sample 1)
The girl is the cookie
[The girl is eating a cookie]          (Marta, Sample 2)
Carolina is for English and Espagnol.
[Carolina speaks English and Spanish] (Marta, Sample 2)

Assuming that [ + uniform ] is the default setting, a problem that arises is how the use of the copula in utterances such as the above should be interpreted. When we consider that the copula in the above sentences is used instead of the relevant main verbs (perhaps because these verbs are not as yet a part of the productive vocabulary), it is apparent that these early utterances are not indicative of parameter setting. Rather, a possible explanation is that children start out with a limited set of verbs which they may then extend to other contexts even if they are inappropriate in terms of the target language. Since as we saw, the *is* copula appears early in the speech of L2 learners, at the early stages, the learners (as in the case of Muriel and Marta) may use it as a sort of universal sentence builder. The MUP, however, fails to account for utterances such as those in (4) as it ignores the possible role that the verbs themselves may play in determining whether the target language is uniformly inflected or not.

Lakshmanan (1993/1994) observes that the copula *is* is the first verb to emerge in Marta's L2 and it typically occurs in the uncontracted form.[2] Lakshmanan also reports that lexical verbs (other than the copula) are nearly always absent in the early stages of Marta's L2 grammar (i.e. in samples 1 and 2). However, unlike what has been reported in the case of L1 English speaking children, Marta does not produce binominal expressions. Instead, in those instances where a transitive verb is omitted, Marta produces a curious construction using the preposition *for* (e.g. *This is the boy for the cookie* [= This is a boy eating a cookie] and *For the Mommy* [= I hear Mommy]. The existence of verbless utterances in the early stages of Marta's L2 poses a problem for Hyams and Safir's (1991) account of the evidence from Marta. As discussed in Chapter 3 (see Note 11), according to Hyams and Safir (1991), even though Marta' use of verb inflections fails to fulfill the 80% criterion and she has already stopped omitting subjects, the evidence from Marta does not diconfirm the MUP since Marta may have known more about English than is indicated by her productions. Specifically, according to Hyams and Safir, Marta may already have determined that English is morphologically non-uniform, but may merely not have mastered all the verb inflections. As reported in chapter 4, the highest percentage of subject omissions are present in sample 1 (64%) and the percentage drops sharply to 17% in sample 2. In both samples, as stated above, lexical verbs other than the copula are rarely present and are omitted where they would be required. Since verbs (other than the copula) are themselves delayed, and since a sharp decrease in the percentage of null subjects was not evidenced in any of the subsequent samples where lexical verbs are present, it would be difficult to conclude (along with Hyams and Safir) that the sharp decrease in null subjects is a result of Marta's having figured out prior to sample 2 that English is not uniform. In addition, the fact that it is probably the simple present tense paradigm of verbs (other than the copula) which would be the crucial trigger for the change from a + uniform setting of the MUP to the -uniform value, also weakens their claims that Marta has probably determined that English is not uniform prior to sample 2. Furthermore, assuming that Hyams and Safir's characterization of the distinction between passive knowledge and active knowledge is fully correct, then in the case of lexical verbs that are omitted, we would have to conclude that Marta does in fact know the particular verbs but simply fails to produce them. As stated in Chapter 3 (see note 11), while Hyams and Safir apply the distinction between passive and active knowledge to Marta's use of inflections, they are careful not use the same criteria with respect to subject omissions in the early grammars of English. If we were to apply the distinction between passive knowledge and active knowledge to Marta's omissions of subjects, then, by the same token, we would have to conclude that even in sample 1, where the highest percentage subject omissions occur, Marta does in fact know that English requires overt subjects but that she fails to obey this knowledge in her actual productions.

A third problem with Jaeggli and Hyams' analysis concerns the acquisition of the different inflections. Our findings indicated that the obligatory uses of inflections are not all learned at the same time but depend on the type of verb morphology. We also found that inflections which involve changes in endings (such as the inflections for the present third person regular and past regular) were not acquired by any of the four subjects, suggesting that saliency plays a role in the acquisition of such inflections. In the context of these findings, it is relevant to mention the findings of a recent study of the longitudinal emergence of verb inflections (- *ing*, -*s*, and -*ed*/IRREG), in four American English speaking children (Bloom, Lifter and Hafitz 1980). The study found that the semantics of the verbs that these children were learning played a major role in their acquisition of verb inflections. These inflections emerged at the same time in these children's speech. However, it was found that the distribution of these inflections varied selectively with different populations of verbs. More specifically, the study found that the probability of a verb being inflected and also the specific type of inflection supplied could be predicted from the relation between the verb and the item that received focus as subject (actor, agent, mover, patient, entity). Evidence was also found for the selective use of inflections; the selective use of inflections was found to be co-extensive with distinctions of verb aspect. In other words, the presence of inflections (and to a certain degree, which inflections) depended partly on the syntax of sentences whereas the selective use of the different inflectional morphemes was largely influenced by the inherent aspectual meaning of the individual verb. These findings serve to stress the important role played by the semantics of verbs in inflection acquisition. In so doing, they also undermine claims underlying purely syntactic proposals (such as the MUP) that the initial omission of inflections in the developing grammars of a morphologically non-uniform language such as English, is a result of a [+ uniform] default setting.

A question that needs to be posed with respect to the learnability problem is: What specifically triggers the discovery that English is [- uniform]? Is it the 3rd person singular regular? the 3rd person singular irregular? the auxiliaries *be*, *do*, and *have* ? Or all of these? Hyams and Jaeggli are silent about the exact nature of the linguistic elements which trigger the change from [+ uniform] to [- uniform]. As we saw above, in the case of Uguisu and Muriel, the inflection for the present third person singular is extended incorrectly to other contexts. In other words, the emergence of this ending does not seem to have made the subjects realize that English is [- uniform] judging by their generalizations.[3] The point is that even if we assume that parameter setting is at work, we would still need to explain how learners work out the language specific facts with respect to tense and agreement markings for the different types of verb morphology. For example, L1 and L2 learners of English will need to determine that in the present tense paradigm, only the third person singular form is inflected and that the other verb forms are uninflected. With respect to the early grammars (and IL grammars) of English, the parameter setting model predicts that when the learners shift from a [+ uniform] stage to a [- uniform] stage, there should be a similar shift in their productions, from a stage where inflections are omitted most of the time to a stage where obligatory inflections are supplied often or most of the time. But as we saw above, the acquisition of verb inflections does not take place suddenly. Instead, it takes place gradually and appears to depend on factors such as the type of verb morphology and inherent semantics of verbs.

A fourth problem concerns the binary distinction made between pro-drop languages and non-pro-drop languages. As discussed in Chapter 3, Hyams and Jaeggli's proposals ignore the possibility that tensed sentences with missing subjects may be present in the child's input. In their account of the pro-drop phenomenon, as in most other accounts, the existence of subjectless utterances in English is not taken into account. Specifically, such accounts fail to account for the learnability problem posed by sentences such as those presented in (5)

> 5. Tastes good.
> Seems O.K. to me.
> Think I'll go home.

Although such sentences may arguably represent a class of nonstandard utterances, such utterances do in fact occur and enter the stream of data a child may use to form her grammar. However, the MUP as in previous accounts of the pro-drop parameter, restricts the domain of pro-drop to Standard English forms. Such proposals are problematic for an account of language acquisition within a framework of parameter setting. As pointed out by Valian (1990), if we assume that null subjects are a universal property of child language, then the occurrence of the above sentences (given the crucial role of simple triggers within this framework), may be construed as positive evidence that English is indeed pro-drop. In other words, such data, may be perceived by the learner as being inconsistent with the licensing condition of the MUP, that is, that null subjects are allowed only in languages that are [+ uniform]. Such data may therefore lead the child to assume that subjects are optional in English.

Moreover, there is the added problem of ellipsis in casual speech. It is conceivable that the child encounters such utterances in the input. How then does the child distinguish between ellipsis and pro-drop? In our own data of the four subjects, there were several cases of ellipsis which were not taken into account when computing the percentage of null subjects since such sentences are acceptable in English. Hyams and Jaeggli do not account for the presence of such data. What we need is a more in depth analysis of how children learning English come to acquire casual speech rules and yet do not generalize the occurrence of null subjects in casual speech to the rest of the grammar. In other words, we need to account for how the potentially destructive processes of casual speech phenomena are circumvented.

As discussed in Chapter 3, Roeper and Weissenborn (1990) present a solution to the learnability problem that is posed by the presence of contradictory data. According to Roeper and Weissenborn, the tensed embedded clause in English functions as a unique trigger in that the learner will never encounter missing subjects in this domain. In contrast to the matrix clause therefore, the evidence in the embedded clause is consistent with only one of the parametric choices. Roeper and Weissenborn suggest that children are sensitive to the unique triggering function of embedded clauses. As stated in Chapter 3, Valian

(1991) found that English speaking children do not omit subjects in tensed embedded clauses, which supports Roeper and Weissenborn's proposals regarding the role of tensed embedded clauses in parameter setting.

A question that may be posed in the context of child L2 acquisition is whether child L2 learners, like child L1 learners, are also similarly sensitive to the unique triggering status of tensed embedded clauses (for a discussion of this issue, see Gass and Lakshmanan 1991). Recall that only three of the child L2 learners (Marta, Cheo and Muriel) omitted subjects whereas Uguisu, the native speaker of Japanese, rarely omitted subjects. The transcripts of Marta, Cheo and Muriel were examined for subject omissions in tensed embedded clauses. The examination revealed that Marta and Cheo never omit subjects in tensed embedded clauses. As for Muriel, referential subjects were never omitted (except for one instance) from tensed embedded clauses. In all, there were only two instances of subject omission from tensed embedded clauses. In one case, the omitted subject was an expletive subject *there* and in the other case the omitted subject was a referential *it*. In both cases, the verb in the embedded clause was the copula *is*. In section 5.1.2, we will show that the apparent subject omission by Muriel in *it is* contexts may be a result of perceptual factors at the phonological/morphological level.[4]

A final problem relates to Hyams' and Jaeggli's proposals regarding the different methods of identification. As we saw earlier, they propose that in early grammars of English and morphologically non-uniform languages, the method of identification is through the topic or null sentence topic (i.e. as in Chinese) whereas the method of identification in the early grammars of richly inflected null subject languages (such as Italian) is through agreement. In Chapter 2, we discussed some of the shortcomings of such proposals for the identification of null subjects. Specifically, we argued that identification through agreement and identification through Topic chaining are not on par since in the former method only the content of the null-subject is specified by the agreement features but not its unique reference which is recovered from the discourse. In the latter method, it is the unique reference of the null subject that is recoverable. Hyams and Jaeggli's proposals ignore what is common to Chinese type and Italian type null subject languages, namely that in both, unique reference is supplied by the discourse context. With respect to the data from Marta and Cheo, we observed in Chapter 3 that contrary to Hilles' (1991) claims, there is no compelling evidence that null subjects in these learners' IL are identified through the Topic or null sentence topic as in Chinese. Claims that null subjects in the early grammars of

English (and other morphologically non-uniform languages) are identified through topic chains, needs to be more fully substantiated. Evidence from the early grammars (and child L2 grammars) of Chinese should throw light on this issue given the fact that the Chinese speaking child, in contrast to the English speaking child, will encounter positive evidence that null-subjects in Chinese are identified through topic chaining. In Chapter 3, we reported on the findings of a recent study by Wang et al (1992) which compared null arguments in the early grammars of Chinese and English. The study found that Chinese speaking children omitted a higher percentage of subjects than English speaking children. Wang et al did not find a subject object asymmetry in the case of the early grammar of Chinese, since the Chinese speaking children also omitted objects. As discussed in Chapter 3, Wang et al propose that there are two parameters at work in the omission of arguments in adult grammars. One parameter, the Null-pronoun parameter, licenses *pro* in the subject position of tensed clauses in languages such as Italian, which have with rich agreement. Another parameter, the Discourse-Oriented parameter (DO) licenses both null subjects and null objects in discourse oriented languages such as Chinese and Japanese, which lack agreement. Null subjects in the matrix clause and null objects, which are both considered as variables by Wang et al, are identified by a Discourse topic. Null subjects in the embedded clause, which are instances of *pro* are identified by the c-commanding nominal. Wang et al propose that the default value of the DOP is [- DO] whereas the default value of the Null-pronoun parameter is [+Null-pronoun]. According to Wang et al, Chinese speaking children will encounter overwhelming positive evidence that Chinese is a discourse oriented language and resetting of the value of the DOP to [+DO] will take place very early resulting in the omission of both subjects and objects. According to Wang et al, English speaking children initially omit subjects because they have initially set the value of the Null pronoun parameter to [+ Null-pronoun]. However, Wang et al's proposal with respect to the status of subjects in the early grammars of English is problematic. During the null subject stage in the early grammars of English (but not in the early grammars of Italian), verb inflections are omitted and as in the case of the adult grammars of English, there is no rich agreement to enable the recovery of the identity of *pro*. In Chapter 3, we suggested a modification of Wang et al's proposals, according to which the initial setting of both the DOP and the Null-pronoun parameter is set at the negative value. Chinese speaking children will reset the value of the DOP on the basis of positive evidence. English speaking children and Italian speaking children will never encounter positive evidence for resetting the value of the DOP to the positive value. As for the Null pronoun parameter, Italian speaking children will encounter overwhelming evidence that Italian has rich agreement and resetting of the value of the Null pronoun parameter to the positive value will take place very early. Chinese speaking children and English speaking children will not encounter positive evidence that Chinese and English have rich agreement and therefore they will remain with the default value, namely [- Null pronoun]. Under this modified proposal, we would have to assume along with Valian (1991) and P.Bloom (1990) that English speaking children know from the very beginning that English requires subjects to be overt in tensed clauses and that their failure to obey this knowledge is a result of performance factors. A question that may be raised in the context of child L2 acquisition is whether child L2 learners of English, regardless of whether their L1 instantiates the positive or the negative value of the DOP and the Null pronoun parameter, will correctly hypothesize from the very beginning that English requires subjects to be overt in tensed clauses. In what follows we will argue that child L2 learners of English do indeed appear to know from the very beginning that English requires subjects of tensed clauses to be obligatorily overt and that their failure to obey this knowledge is a result of perceptual factors that are not related to parameter setting.

*5.1.2. Perceptual Factors and the L1*

The findings of our study indicated that the theoretical construct of the MUP is supported only in the case of Cheo. The other three subjects do not offer any evidence that the MUP and the null subject phenomenon are related. However, we still need to account for the following. (i) The omission of subjects in Marta's and Muriel's IL. (ii) the consistent failure to omit subjects (except for three cases) on the part of Uguisu. We will argue here that the interaction between perceptual factors and the L1 may be responsible for the above results. We will also suggest that regardless of whether or not the L1 requires overt subjects, child L2 learners of English probably know from the very beginning that English is a non-null subject language.

Let us first consider Marta. Our findings indicate that the *is* context is a strong predictor of the occurrence of null subjects in Marta's IL. Why should this be the case? As we will demonstrate below, the relationship between *is* contexts and null subjects appears to be the result of a phonological matching between the English *it's*, and *is* with the Spanish copula *es* (for a similar proposal regarding the interlingual identification between English *it's*, and *is* and the

Spanish *es* see Cancino et al 1974). A characterization of the null subject phenomenon in Marta's interlanguage is presented in figure 5.1.

**Stage 1:**

| English | Spanish | Triggers transfer | Subjects omitted | Weak generalization |
|---|---|---|---|---|
| *It's* | | to L2 grammar | in *it is* | to other verbs |
| ↓ | *Es* ---------> | of English ---------> | contexts ---------> | and pronouns |
| *Is* | | | | |

**Stage 2:**

| English | | Null subjects | Generalization |
|---|---|---|---|
| *It's* | | abandoned in | to other verbs |
| ↓ | ---------> | *It is* contexts ---------> | and pronouns |
| *It is* | | | |

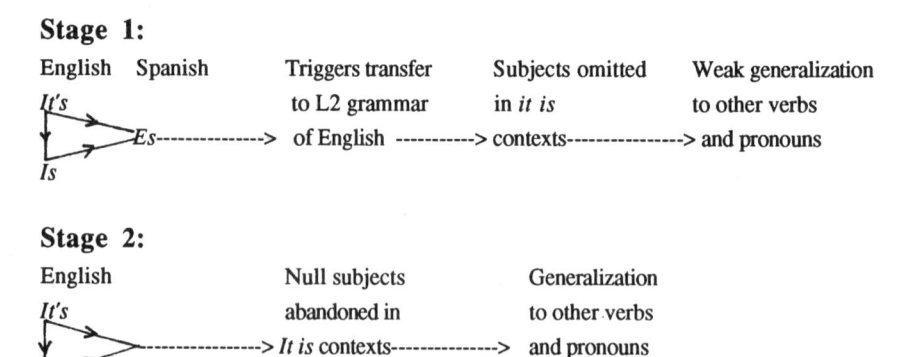

*Fig. 5.1. Characterization of the null-subject phenomenon in Marta's IL*

As we saw in Chapter 4, initially (i.e. in sample 1) null subjects are largely restricted to copula *is* contexts (specifically *it is* contexts). This suggests that perhaps the English *it's* is perceived as *is* /Spanish *es*. This leads to an association between *it's*, *is* and Spanish *es*. The fact that *es* is a copula in Spanish may also have caused Marta to hypothesize that subjects in English can be dropped in *is* contexts.[5] However, since this hypothesis is only weakly extended to *non-is* contexts and contexts requiring a subject pronoun other than *it*, it suggests that Marta may indeed know from the very beginning that English requires subjects of tensed clauses to be overt. Later, when *it's* is correctly analyzed as consisting of two constituents, that is, *it* and *is*, it triggers a realization that unlike in Spanish, subjects cannot be dropped in *is* contexts. Thus null subjects are abandoned from *it is* contexts and this generalization is extended to the context of other verbs and pronouns. As discussed earlier, Marta never omitted subjects from tensed embedded clauses, even in those cases where the verbal element is the copula *is* and the subject is the pronoun *it*. This fact further strengthens the view that the subject omissions in the early stages of Marta's IL may not be the result of an incorrect parameter setting and that she may know from the very beginning that English requires overt subjects.

Let us now examine the evidence from the data which support the above conclusion. There are no instances of the subject pronoun *it* (either referential or expletive) in samples 1 and 2 (see examples in (6)). As (7) illustrates, the first two instances of *it* occur in sample 3 and in both cases the verbal element is the copula (uncontractible form). What is interesting is that tensed embedded clauses first emerge in sample 3 and the subjects of these embedded clauses are always overtly realized (for discussion regarding the emergence of tensed embedded clauses in Marta's IL see Lakshmanan and Selinker 1994).

    6.    Is mine.
           /Iss/ the bear.
           Is basketball ?
           Is going in the floor.
           No is wet.
           Is no going to rain there in Puerto Rico.

    7.    Here it is.
           I don't know what it is.

Recall that the sudden decrease in the percentage of subject omissions (from 64% to 17%) takes place in the previous sample, that is sample 2. It may be that Marta's successful analysis of English *it's* may have been completed prior to sample 3, that is, around the time period represented by sample 2. In addition, the fact that subjects are always overtly realized in Marta's earliest productions of the tensed embedded clauses which first emerge in sample 3, suggests that Marta may have had access to knowledge about the unique triggering status of the embedded clause domain.

In sample 4, *It's* makes its appearance (see examples in (8)). In fact there are several instances of *it's* in sample 4. In addition, in sample 4, there is one occurrence of Subject-verb inversion (yes/no question) where *is* and *it* are separated.

    8.    It's a little bigger.
           It's coke.
           It's eating the coke.
           It's your turn now.
           Is it bigger?

Subject-verb (copula) inversion in direct Wh questions, where the subject is *it* (*What is it?*) occurs first in sample 6 and it later occurs three times in a row in sample 7. Expletive *it* makes its first appearance in sample 9, and is overtly realized even in tensed embedded clauses.

9. Never go out when it's cold.
   In my pants it's not hot.

As we discussed in Chapter 4, the percentage of subject omissions drops by more than 45 points in sample 2. There is some fluctuation between samples 3 and 6, and except for sample 4 (where subjects are omitted around 30% of the time) subject omissions in samples 3, 5 and 6 never exceed 21%. What is interesting is that similar fluctuation is not observed from sample 7 onwards as the percentage of null subjects never goes above 9.2%. As stated earlier, it is from sample 7 onwards that tensed embedded clauses, (which first emerged in sample 3), become more productive. As in the case of Marta's earliest tensed embedded clauses, subjects are always overtly supplied in these later occurrences of embedded clauses.

Let us now examine the relation between *is* contexts and null subjects in Cheo's IL. When we examine the early transcripts of Cheo, we find that *is* contexts do not appear to be playing a role in Cheo's omission of subjects. Subjects are rarely deleted in *is* contexts, which suggests that Cheo in contrast to Marta, does not associate *it's*, and *is* with Spanish *es* as the examples in (10) from the earliest sample when Cheo began to produce English indicate.

10a. E:   What do you say in Spanish for that? It's a apple?
     Cheo: (He) no apple.           (Cheo, sample 3)

  b. E:   Is this an apple?
     Cheo: No este is no apple.    (No, this is not an apple)
                                    (Cheo, sample 3)

The highest percentage of subject omissions occurs in sample 3, but the percentage of subject omissions is considerably lower (only 20%) when compared to Marta's subject omissions in the earliest sample when she began to produce English. Moreover, the fact that this percentage is accounted for by only two instances out of a total of 10 utterances, and also given the fact that subsequent to this sample subject omissions never go above 10%, renders weak the position that Cheo's initial hypothesis is consistent with English being a null subject language. The transcripts of Cheo were manually searched for instances of tensed embedded clauses. The search revealed that tensed embedded clauses first emerge in sample 6 and in this and in subsequent samples, subjects are always overtly supplied in this domain, suggesting that as in case of Marta, Cheo

# DISCUSSION AND CONCLUSIONS

may have had access to the knowledge about the unique triggering status of tensed embedded clauses.

It is relevant to mention here that there is evidence from the transcripts of Cheo that in the early samples he was receiving ungrammatical input from the experimenter (a native speaker of English). Specifically, included among these occurrences of ungrammatical input are instances of subject omissions which would not be acceptable even in colloquial English. As stated in Chapter 4, Cheo went through a nearly five month long silent period and did not produce any English in the first two samples. It is felt that the ungrammatical input directed to Cheo may have been an instance of the experimenter's efforts to "accommodate" to Cheo, in order to aid comprehension and foster communication. These instances of ungrammatical input occur mainly in the early samples. The examples in (11) illustrate the ungrammatical input involving subject omissions that occurred in sample 3, which represents Cheo's first attempts at producing English. The relevant instances of ungrammatical input involving missing subjects are underlined (for a detailed discussion of this issue see Gass and Lakshmanan 1991).

11a. Native Speaker (NS): What's he eating?
Cheo (C): Uh.
NS: What's that ?
C: Una cos con leche [something with milk]
NS: What?
C: Cosa Comer [something eat]
NS: Talk loud because we have to hear you.
C: Una cosa coma. Una cosa comer
[something eat]
NS: It's a apple.
C: Apple?
NS: Um.
C: No.
NS: What do you say in Spanish for that? It's a apple?
C: (He) no apple.
NS: It's not an apple?
C: No.
NS: Oh, hum ah, may, I don't know what it is? <u>Is apple?</u>

|      |     |                                                                          |
|------|-----|--------------------------------------------------------------------------|
|      | C:  | No. oop.                                                                 |
| 11b. | NS: | So, hay, tell me about your sister, does she ahm, does she, she doesn't speak English? |
|      | C:  | No.                                                                      |
|      | NS: | Does she speak Spanish?                                                  |
|      | C:  | No.                                                                      |
|      | NS: | Nothing?                                                                 |
|      | C:  | No.                                                                      |
|      | NS: | She doesn't talk? Always quiet? <u>No No, No talk</u>?                   |
|      | C:  | Que cuando, cuando yo alla, no. Verdad coli que usted si habla. Vervad? Di. [ That when over, over there I was, no.Isn't it true, isn't it true, coli, that you can talk? Right? Say.] |
|      | NS: | No tongue, no?                                                           |
|      | C:  | uh hum. Se la comio la lengua un, la cucaracha [ A cockroach ate her tongue]. |

While it may not be valid to emphasize the role of such ungrammatical input, at the same time, we cannot rule out the possibility that such input may have contributed (even to a small degree), to Cheo's omission of subjects in sample 3. However, what is interesting is that subject omissions in the input provided by the native speaker experimenter are restricted to matrix clauses and subjects are never omitted in the tensed embedded clause domain. The fact that Cheo also never omits subjects from tensed embedded clauses also suggests that like Marta, he may have known from the very beginning that English requires subjects to be overt and that the omission of subjects in sample 3, which is the first sample that Cheo produced utterances in English, may be related to performance factors along with the added factor of contradictory input.

Let us now consider Muriel. We stated in Chapter 4 that apparent subject omission in Muriel's IL appears to be the result of her attempts to analyze *it's*. In fact, except for one instance, all the occurrences of null subjects are restricted to *it is/it's* constructions. *It's* first occurs in sample 1 and 2. In sample 3, this is replaced by *ist* which, as pointed out by Gerbault (1978) may be the result of phonological interference from French since French has the /st/ but not the /ts/ combination. In sample 4, *is* and *iste* are added and they coexist along with *ist* until sample 9.

## DISCUSSION AND CONCLUSIONS 135

    12.    Ist going to sleep
              Is very good.
              Iste mine

*Ist* and *iste* appear to be allomorphs of *is* as they occur in *This is* constructions and with the pronoun *he* as the examples in (13) indicate.

    13.    This is
              This ist
              Thist
              This iste
              He'st a bad boy

The allomorphs *ist* and *iste* do not occur in samples 9 through 17. Only *is* is present and in nearly all the cases the subject (*it/there*) is omitted. This is illustrated by the examples in (14).

    14.    Is just a picture of it.
              Ya, because is here.
              Is going the other way.
              I know is some more.
              But is not a tree, I know.

In sample 8, there are two cases of *it's* and in both instances *it's* is used instead of *it*.

    15.    You put it's here
              You know it's means?

In samples 9 through 17 there are also cases where *is* s used instead of *it*.

    16.    Is will be good.
              Is could do.
              Because is was eleven, right?

It may be argued that the analysis of *it's* and the omission of subjects in *is* contexts is peculiar to Muriel and may not be true of other French speakers learning English. However, there is evidence to show that this is not the case. In a recent longitudinal study, Tiphine (1983) found that two of her French speaking subjects (nine-year-old Jean and eleven-year-old Patrick) consistently dropped subjects in the context of *is* in their English. However, the percentage of such omissions was much higher than in Muriel's IL. Omission of subjects in *is* contexts persisted up to the very last stage of the data collection. Further, one of the subjects (Patrick) also went through a stage when he used *it* for *is* (that is, the reverse of what we saw in the case of Muriel).

As stated earlier, Muriel never omitted referential subjects (except for one instance) in tensed embedded clauses. There were only two instances where the subject of a tensed embedded clause was omitted. In one case, the omitted subject was an expletive subject *there* and in the second case the omitted subject was a referential *it*. In both cases, the verb in the embedded clause was the copula *is*. The evidence from the tensed embedded clauses produced by Muriel when considered along with the evidence that her subject omissions in *it is* contexts is probably related to her phonological/morphological analysis of *it's*, indicates that as in the case of Marta and Cheo, she may have know early on that English is not a null subject language.

Let us now turn to Uguisu, the native speaker of Japanese. According to Jaeggli and Hyams (1988), children acquiring a [- uniform] language such as English, start out by treating English as Chinese and move towards a stage when they treat English as English. Japanese is like Chinese (with respect to the identification requirement), so we would expect Uguisu to move from a point where she treats English as Japanese to a point where she treats English as English. Although Uguisu omits inflections, she rarely omits subjects. In all there were only three occurrences of null subjects and none of these instances involved the subject position of the tensed embedded clause. Subjects, in short, appear to be salient to her. Even in the earliest samples we find instances of expletive *it.*. For example, we saw in Chapter 4 that she has problems in supplying the inflectional endings for past regular and the present third person regular. We also stated that the earliest samples contain a large number of copula utterances but in contrast to Marta and Muriel, Uguisu does not have any problems in producing *it's*. As in the case of subjects, objects are also rarely omitted in Uguisu's IL.[6]

In Chapter 2, we saw that in Japanese, as in other discourse oriented languages, null subjects as well as null objects occur. Uguisu appears to be using what Sharwood Smith (1988) has referred to as the "non-equivalence strategy". This is the converse of the equivalence strategy scenario where the learner makes an initial assumption of L1/L2 structural equivalence and initially rejects evidence that confirms this. In the non-equivalence strategy scenario, the learner

## DISCUSSION AND CONCLUSIONS 137

adopts an "exotic" view of the target language initially assuming its structure to be structurally distinct from that of the L1. In other words, Uguisu must have perceived that English is very different from Japanese and that it requires obligatorily overt subjects (and objects). As a result, subjects and objects are rarely dropped in Uguisu's IL. The transcripts on Uguisu were examined for the existence of topic-comment structures, as this would suggest that Uguisu views English as being similar to Japanese. However, no instances of topic comment structures could be found in the early samples and there were hardly any topic comment structures in the later samples. In this connection it is relevant to mention that many of Uguisu's early utterances are of the *This is a* ---- type. Hakuta (1974) has referred to Uguisu's use of this form as an instance of a prefabricated pattern. In fact, as Hakuta has shown, prefabricated patterns, at least in the initial stages of learning constituted a significant proportion of Uguisu's early utterances. This may also have been partly responsible for the non-occurrence of null subjects in Uguisu's IL. Further, one cannot rule out the possibility that frequent use of utterances of the *This is a* --- type may have contributed to the saliency of obligatory subjects in English.

According to Jaeggli and Hyams, null subjects in the early grammars of English are merely an effect of the [+ uniform] setting of the MUP. An implication of this claim is that the null subject phenomenon in the early grammars of English is not an effect of factors external to UG. However, if we assume with Jaeggli and Hyams that the null subject phenomenon is simply an epiphenomenon and not a parameter in itself (as has been proposed previously), then, there would be nothing to prevent it from being triggered by other factors, including factors that are not considered a part of UG. As we have seen above, perceptual factors play an important role in the occurrence of null subjects in Marta's and Muriel's IL and the non-occurrence of null subjects in Uguisu's IL. In the case of Marta, we saw that perceptual factors (involving certain language specific facts of L1 and L2) appear to be responsible for her use of an equivalence strategy in a restricted structural context. In Uguisu's case, perceptual factors encourage the use of a non-equivalence strategy. Perceptual factors initially lead to the deletion of subjects in Marta's IL in the restricted domain of *is* contexts and to the consistent inclusion of subjects in Uguisu's IL. In the case of Muriel, perceptual factors are responsible for her misanalysis of *it's*, which in turn leads to what appears to be on the surface at least, omission of subjects in *it is* contexts. Cheo was the only subject who provided evidence for the MUP. However, we also found that in sample 3, which is the first sample in which

Cheo produced utterances in English and is also the sample where the highest percentage of subject omissions occur, the input provided by the native speaker experimenter also included utterances where the subject had been omitted. In addition, we noticed a weak involvement between *is* contexts and subject omissions in sample 7 for Cheo. This, along with the evidence from the other subjects, suggests that one cannot attribute the null subject phenomenon to a single factor, namely the MUP.

Furthermore, the finding that Marta, Cheo and Uguisu never drop subjects from tensed embedded clauses and that Muriel's omission of subjects in this domain consisted of only two instances, one of which involved the *it is* context and the other the *there* (expletive) *is* context, suggests that all four subjects probably knew from the very earliest stages that English requires subjects of tensed clauses to be obligatorily overt.

### 5.1.3. Individual Differences

Hyams and others have observed that the null subject phenomenon is a universal property of child language. However, in the case of the four child subjects, we found that even though they proceed through a stage when they omit inflections they exhibit considerable variation in regard to the extent to which they omit subjects. We saw for example that null subjects hardly ever occur in Uguisu's IL. Even in regard to the other three learners, we did not find evidence for a common strategy/principle underlying the subjects' use of null subjects.

The potential importance of individual differences has been acknowledged by Geschwind (1980) and Peters (1983) among others. It is commonly believed that development of language is remarkably uniform across children. However, as Peters has demonstrated, children do not all follow the same paths on the way to language acquisition-- at least with respect to the kinds of utterances they produce. While there may be major uniformities, there may also be many variations on this basic pattern, determined by individual differences. As Peters has stated, individual differences, among other factors may explain many of the observed strategy differences among children learning their first language. We will argue here that individual differences may be important in explaining variation in the IL development of second language learners as well.

Individual differences may result from the differences in what learners perceive. In the case of Marta, for example, we find that a phonological matching between *it's* and *is* and Spanish *es* triggers her omission of subjects in

English. At first, null subjects occur mostly in *is* contexts and are later weakly extended to the context of other verbs and pronouns other than *it*.[7] On the other hand, in the case of Cheo, there is no evidence that he makes a similar early association between the Spanish copula *es* and *it's* and *is* in English. Initially, null subjects rarely occur in *is* contexts. In the case of Muriel, we find that null subjects are restricted to *it is* (and also *there is*) contexts and do not generalize to other verbs or pronouns. As we saw above, null subjects in *is* contexts in the case of Muriel appear to be related to her attempts in analyzing the constituents of *it's*. As for Uguisu, we noticed that a non-equivalence strategy may be at work, which may explain why null subjects rarely occur in her IL. It is possible that this strategy of non-equivalence is a general one, in which case, we would expect it to operate in all domains. On the other hand, this strategy may be limited to certain domains. If the latter holds, it would be of interest to investigate the differences, if any, in its use with respect to UG principles (i.e. core grammar) as opposed to the peripheral aspects of language.

Another reason for the variation observed with respect to the four subjects has to do with different speaking demands. For adult second language acquisition, it has been hypothesized (White 1985a, 1985b) that when the parameter setting in the L1 is different from the L2, the L1 setting is transferred to the L2. In this context, it is interesting to note that silent periods have been reported only for child L2 learners but not for adults. It may be that children acquiring an L2, unlike adults, go through what may be called (for want of a better term) " a hold stage". Children may initially go through a "hold stage" during which the L1 structures and (settings) are filtered and do not automatically transfer to the developing L2 grammar, unless positive evidence in the L2 input indicates that the L2 matches the L1 with respect to the particular property. Adult learners in contrast, face greater communicative demands and so as a result, the L1 settings and structures may be transferred directly to the IL.

All the four subjects in this study went through an initial silent period (during which we hypothesize the "hold stage" is operative). However, the four subjects varied with respect to the length of this silent period. Marta began to produce English after one month of exposure to English. In contrast, Cheo, had nearly a five month silent period. Even during the first two sample periods, he consistently failed to respond in English even when requested and instead preferred to use only Spanish. Muriel, the native speaker of French, also went through a four month silent period. As Gerbault (1978) has reported, Muriel's production during the first three months was close to zero, even though she was at that time attending an English speaking nursery school. Interestingly enough, her first attempts at producing English coincided with the period when she began attending a bilingual French/English school. As for Uguisu, we stated in Chapter 4, that she was allowed to speak in English when she was ready and she went through a five month silent period. A trip that she went on with her family during which she was accompanied by an American adult (English speaking) may have acted as a catalyst. When she returned from the trip, as Hakuta (1975) has reported, she suddenly began to speak in English. Her first attempts at speaking were in a play situation with her peers.

We stated above that during the "hold stage" or the silent period, the L1 settings/structures are not transferred to the developing L2 grammar. Why then do we find that in the case of Marta, there is an association between the Spanish copula and *its* and *is* in English? It may be that during the early samples Marta may have been forced to produce English before she was ready for it. As a result, her own early productions of English utterances (specifically *it's* which she always rendered as *is*) may have influenced her perception of the input. The apperceived input (Gass 1988) in turn may have triggered the omission of subjects in this restricted domain, even though she may have known that English is not a null subject language. The nature of the trigger will probably determine the nature of the consequences in the IL. As we noticed in the case of Marta, the phonological matching between *is*, *its* and *es* triggers the use of null subjects in English. But perhaps because the trigger is phonological, it does not have serious effects. In the case of Cheo, although he has the same L1 as Marta, there is no such phonological trigger. As we may recall, Cheo went through a much longer silent period when compared to Marta. Perhaps because of this longer silent period Cheo's early English speech (at least with respect to *it's* utterances) did not have the same destructive effects with respect to his perception of *it's*. Instead, as stated earlier, Cheo appears to have perceived the difference between *it's*, *is* and Spanish *es* during the "hold stage". In the case of Uguisu, we stated that she appears to have perceived that English is typologically very different than Japanese (i.e. with respect to null subjects). As Huang (1984) has stated, Japanese is a discourse-oriented language where null objects and null subjects occur. This is in contrast to English, which is a sentence oriented language. Subjects appear to be salient to Uguisu and she hardly ever drops them. This perception may have been promoted during the long silent period. When the L1 is perceived as being typologically very different from the L2, transfer from the L1 to the developing L2 grammar may be blocked. On the other hand, if she had been forced to speak in English before she was ready to do so, it is possible that it may have caused her to use an equivalence strategy in order to meet the increased communicative demands. In this case, we would expect her to drop both subjects and objects in her English L2.

*5.1.4. Implications for Access to UG in Child SLA*

In Chapter 1 we outlined three situations that may obtain with respect to access to UG in SLA. The three scenarios are the direct access scenario, indirect access scenario and the no access scenario. In the direct access situation, the L2 learner, like the child L1 learner has direct access to the principles of UG. In the indirect access situation, the L2 learner's IL is constrained by UG (as in the direct access scenario), with one difference in that the L1 is not ignored. In the no access situation, the principles of UG are no longer available to the L2 learner. The IL may serve as an initial template, but where the L1 parametric values differ from the L2, resetting cannot occur. Instead the L2 learner's IL gradually approximates to the L2 through the use of non-UG mechanisms.

The question that needs to be addressed is: Is there evidence from the IL of the four subjects that they are accessing the MUP, which has been posited as a principle of UG? We saw that of the four subjects, only Cheo offers evidence (albeit weak evidence) that the MUP and the null subject phenomenon are related. Similar results were not obtained in the case of the other three subjects. How then do we resolve the issue of access to UG? As we may recall, Hilles (1989) found that Cheo and Marta provide strong evidence in support of the MUP's predictions. This is in contrast to the findings of our study. None of our subjects, with the exception of Cheo gave evidence in support of the MUP. As we observed earlier, the differences in the findings of the two studies may be the result of the differences in our methods of analysis. There appear to be essentially two opposing solutions to the problem posed by the differences between the findings of Hilles (1989) and the study reported here.

Let us consider the first solution which depends crucially on our assumption that the MUP is a principle of UG. Let us therefore assume, for the sake of argument, that the MUP is a UG principle as Hyams and Jaeggli have claimed. Since out of our four subjects, only Cheo provided (weak) evidence for the MUP, we would have to conclude that only Cheo has access to the MUP, and hence to UG, while the other subjects do not. But we would still need to explain why three of our child L2 subjects failed to access this UG principle. It may be argued that other factors (external to UG), such as the perceptual factors discussed above, are partly or wholly responsible for the failure on the part of the three subjects to access the MUP; in other words, that perceptual factors may operate in such a way that access to UG is blocked. Further, it may be argued that the existence of non-natural features in these learners' IL is evidence that their L2 acquisition is not UG constrained. For example, in Muriel's case we found that null subjects are restricted to (referential and non-referential) *it is* contexts; In Marta's IL, there is an initial restriction of null subjects to *it is* contexts which are later weakly extended to other contexts. In Uguisu's case, we found that even during the stage when she omits inflections, she consistently supplies subjects. In terms of the predictions of the MUP, we would not expect such features to occur in any natural language. So we would have to conclude that Marta, Muriel and Uguisu represent the no access scenario.

A major problem involved in drawing this conclusion is that if we conclude that there is no evidence that Marta, Muriel and Uguisu are accessing UG, we would also be led to predict that that they will have limited success in acquiring the L2. However, this conclusion would fail to be borne out as even a cursory glance at the final transcripts of these subjects will indicate. Further, as we saw in our discussion of the implications of our findings for the theory proposed by Jaeggli and Safir, the theoretical construct of the MUP is not without its share of problems, chief among them being that it makes certain incorrect predictions and fails to make certain predictions with respect to our L2 data (including the data from Cheo). The problems that our data pose for the MUP thus render Hyams' and Jaeggli's claims regarding language development questionable.

The second solution derives from the notion that the universal status claimed for the MUP is suspect. In other words, that the MUP is not a principle of UG since its predictions were not supported in the case of three subjects. As we saw earlier, although the MUP received support in the case of Cheo, his acquisition of the obligatory uses of inflections failed to reach the criterion for all the different types of verb morphology except for the copula. On the other hand, the other three subjects appeared to have fared better in comparison with Cheo. How then do we explain the fact that the MUP's predictions were supported in Cheo's case? It could be argued that the MUP is not needed to explain Cheo's IL and that it would not be possible to maintain a UG position for the MUP in light of the data from the other subjects.

In what follows, we will argue that Lillo-Martin's (1991) and Wang et al's (1992) recent claims that there are two parameters (namely, the Discourse oriented Parameter and the Null Pronoun parameter) that are associated with the

## DISCUSSION AND CONCLUSIONS 143

null subject phenomenon, are probably correct and can enable us to account for the child L2 facts observed here. It is relevant to restate here, that while Wang et al appear to be essentially correct in claiming that the default setting of the DOP is set at the value [-DO], their claims that the initial setting for the Null pronoun parameter is set at the positive value may not be accurate (see Chapter 3, section 3.2). Instead, it may be that the setting for both the DOP and the Null pronoun parameter is initially set at the negative value. Let us assume that this is indeed the case. In what follows we explore the consequences of such an assumption in the context of child L2 acquisition of a non-null subject language such as English.

The evidence from our study of the four child L2 learners' developing grammars of English suggest that they appear to know from the very beginning that English requires overt subjects. Subject omissions that do occur appear to be caused by perceptual factors, which are non-UG related. First let us consider the native speakers of Spanish acquiring English as the L2. With respect to the DOP, their L1 (i.e. Spanish) instantiates the negative setting (which, we assume is also the default setting). Since they will never encounter any evidence in the L2 (i.e. English) to warrant a resetting of the [-DO] value to the [+DO], they will remain with the option that is instantiated in the L1. However, with respect to the Null pronoun parameter, the L1 instantiates the value [+ Null pronoun]. As stated above, we depart from Wang et al's analysis in claiming that the default setting for the Null pronoun parameter is also consistent with the negative value. We also hypothesize that in the case of child L2 learners, default settings of a relevant parameter are operative every time the acquisition of a second language is begun. In other words, with respect to the Null pronoun parameter, the Spanish speakers' initial assumption about English would be that it is a [-Null pronoun] language. Recall that even though Marta initially drops subjects, we noticed that it is largely restricted to *is* contexts, which is a result of her misanalysis of *it's* and not the result of a missetting of the value of the Null pronoun parameter. Furthermore, neither Marta nor Cheo drop subjects in tensed embedded clauses, which further indicates that they both know that English requires overt subjects. Since unlike their L1, English does not have rich agreement, positive evidence, which would necessitate a resetting to the positive value, will never be encountered in the input.

Let us now turn to the native speaker of French acquiring English as the L2. With respect to both the DOP and the Null Pronoun parameter, the L1 (i.e. French), like the L2, instantiates the negative value, which as we stated above, is also consistent with the default setting. Therefore, a French speaking child's initial assumption about English would be that English is neither a Discourse oriented language nor a Null pronoun language. Since no evidence to the contrary will be encountered in the input, the French L2 learner of English will remain with the value initially selected. As we saw earlier, Muriel's subject omissions are restricted to *it is* contexts and reflect the problems that she was having at the phonological and morphological level with the element *it's* and are not the result of setting either of the two parameters at a value that is incorrect for English.

Let us now turn to a different scenario, that of a native speaker of Japanese acquiring English as the L2. Japanese instantiates the positive value of the DOP and therefore subjects and objects can be dropped in this language. However, since it lacks agreement, it instantiates the negative value of the Null pronoun parameter. As stated earlier, the default setting for both parameters is consistent with the negative value. So native speakers of Japanese acquiring English as the L2 will initially hypothesize that English is a [-DO] [-Null pronoun] language. But since positive evidence will not be encountered which would necessitate a change in the initial setting, they will remain with the value initially selected. As we saw in the case of the Uguisu, she hardly ever dropped subjects (or objects).

## 5.2. Conclusion

In this study, we tested the predictions of the MUP in the context of child SLA. Specifically, we examined the IL of four children (two native speakers of Spanish, one native speaker of French, and one native speaker of Japanese) who acquired English as a second language in a naturalistic setting. Our findings did not indicate strong evidence for the MUP. In other words, except in the case of Cheo, the native speaker of Spanish, the IL of the other subjects (Marta, Muriel and Uguisu) failed to support Hyams and Jaeggli's claims for a developmental relation between verb inflections and null subjects. Instead, our findings suggested that for these three subjects, perceptual factors may have been responsible for the IL facts that were observed. We demonstrated that *is* contexts are responsible for the occurrence of null subjects in the IL of Marta and Muriel. In the case of Marta, we hypothesized that her use of null subjects is a result of her perception of *it's* and *is* as Spanish *es*. In the case of Muriel, we showed that the restriction of null subjects in *is* contexts is a result of her attempts to determine the constituents of *it's*. As for Uguisu, we found that although her L1 (Japanese)

## DISCUSSION AND CONCLUSIONS

is a null subject language, she rarely omitted subjects. We attributed these results to her use of a non-equivalence strategy.

We discussed the problems posed for learnability theory by the presence of contradictory data in the input. Given the important role of triggering data within a theory of parameter setting (at least in those frameworks which espouse the continuity hypothesis), it would be difficult to ignore the possibility that subjectless utterances that occur in colloquial speech could cause the child to assume that English is a null subject language. Yet, as we discussed earlier, many of the studies which examined the null subject phenomenon in L1 (and L2) acquisition, failed to address the problem of casual speech and it is only recently that the problem posed by contradictory input is beginning to be addressed. The analysis of the IL grammars of the four child L2 subjects indicated support for Roeper and Weissenborn's (1990) proposal that tensed embedded clauses function as a unique trigger in that they do not contain ambiguous information, and that children have access to the knowledge about the unique trigger status of the embedded clause domain.

We showed that the claims for a universal status for the MUP are questionable. Following Lillo-Martin (1991) and Wang et al (1992), we proposed that the null subject phenomenon in adult grammars may actually involve two different parameters: the DOP and the Null Pronoun Parameter. Unlike Lillo-Martin and Wang et, however, we hypothesized that the default setting for both parameters is consistent with the negative value. We also hypothesized that regardless of the setting instantiated in the L1, in the case of child L2 acquisition, the default settings associated with these two parameters are the values that are initially selected by learners. We showed how the modified version of Lillo-Martin's and Wang et al's proposals is successful in explaining the IL facts that were observed with respect to the four child L2 subjects.

Further research with a larger number of child L2 subjects is needed to verify the findings of this study that there is no strong evidence for the posited relation between development of verb morphology and use of null subjects. Further, we need to examine the extent to which the modified version of Lillo-Martin's and Wang et al's proposals concerning the DOP and the Null pronoun parameter receive support in the case of other child L2 acquisition situations, involving second languages other than English and first languages other than the ones considered here.

The study reported here addressed a small range of selected questions concerning what is essentially one of the numerous issues in child second language acquisition. In conclusion, a quotation from Muriel, one of the subjects considered in our study is particularly appropriate. In one of her many exceptional moments, Muriel declared confidently, "I know every language." While the logical problem of first language acquisition has received considerable attention, the problem as it applies to children acquiring a second/third language has not received the attention it deserves. The present study, it is hoped will lead to a greater interest in accounting for how children come to 'know' a language/languages other than their first.

## Notes to Chapter 5

1. It may be argued that the NP *people* may not be analyzed as plural in Uguisu's IL, in which case the third person singular marking would be appropriate. However, all the utterances in (2) occurred in the later samples and not in the early ones. In addition, we notice that Uguisu generalizes the third person singular marking even when the subject is the third person plural pronoun.

2. According to Lakshmanan (1993/1994), the copula, in the early stages of Marta's L2 grammar functions as a place holder for the tense and agreement features of INFL. Lakshmanan provides detailed evidence that the functional category of INFL and the Case Filter principle are operative from the very beginning in the developing English L2 grammar of Marta. Lakshmanan and Selinker (1994) argue that the functional category of C and its maximal projection CP is present from the very earliest stages in the L2 grammars of Muriel and Marta. Grondin and White (1993) also provide detailed evidence that the functional projections of DP (Determiner Phrase), IP and CP are available from the very beginning in the L2 grammars of English speaking children acquiring French as L2. In Chapter 3, we mentioned that in the context of L1 grammars of English, some researchers such as Radford (1990) and Guilfoyle (1984) have attributed the missing subject phenomenon to the non-availability of functional projections. The evidence cited above regarding the status of functional categories and related mechanisms in Child L2 grammars suggests that subject omissions in the case of the child L2 subjects considered in this study (i.e. Marta, Muriel and Cheo) cannot be attributed to the non-availability of functional categories and related mechanisms.

3. In this connection, it is relevant to mention that it is not fully clear from Jaeggli's and Safir's (1989) analysis whether (strictly speaking) the notion of uniformity applies across the different paradigms in a given language or whether a language can be said to instantiate the [+uniform] setting in the case of the verb paradigm in one tense but not another. In English, for example, while the present tense paradigm is non-uniform, the past tense paradigm is [+ uniform]. Yet English, because of the way the remaining paradigms work, counts as a morphologically non-uniform language. The morpholog-

# DISCUSSION AND CONCLUSIONS 147

ical structure of the past tense paradigm can be misleading to the learners in that it may cause them to conclude that English is a uniformly inflected language (at least with respect to the past tense paradigm). Thus we would expect L1 and L2 learners of English to pro-drop in those cases where the past tense is instantiated. (Deshpande, personal communication).

4. Gass and Lakshmanan (1991) suggest that adult L2 learners, unlike child L1 learners and child L2 learners, may not be sensitive to the unique triggering status of embedded clauses. In support of their claims, they cite the findings of White's (1985b) study of the pro-drop parameter in adult L2 acquisition. Crucially, the Spanish speaking subjects in White's study accepted English sentences with missing subjects in tensed embedded clauses. Lakshmanan (1986) also found evidence that adult Japanese ESL learners tended to accept ungrammatical English sentences where the subject of the tensed embedded clause had been deleted.

5. Wong-Fillmore (1976) reports on the unitary perception of a community formula by one of her Spanish speaking subjects. The community in question was the school and the formulaic phrase was *it's recess*. Her seven-year-old subject Jesus, always condensed it to *s'briseh*. This illustrates the problem faced by children in identifying actual speech units.

6. A recent study (Kuriya 1985) of adult Japanese speakers learning English as L2 found that learners at the beginning level rarely dropped subjects or objects.

7. It is relevant to mention here that the variety of Spanish that Marta (and her parents speak) is Puerto Rican Spanish. It has been shown (Hochberg 1986) that in Puerto Rican Spanish the deletion of the /s/ ending from 2sg verb forms has resulted in exceptionally high use of subject pronouns, especially with those verb forms rendered ambiguous by /s/ deletion. However, the loss of the /s/ ending does not result in a non-uniform verb paradigm, as the verb forms in a given paradigm are still uniformly inflected. This raises an interesting question regarding how the increased use of overt subjects in her L1 may have influenced Marta's developing L2.

# References

Adams, M. 1978. "Methodology for Examining Second Language Acquisition". *Second Language Acquisition: A Book of Readings* ed. by E.Hatch, 277-296. Rowley, Massachusetts: Newbury House.

Adjemian, C. 1976. "On the Nature of Interlanguage Systems". *Language Learning* 26.297-320.

Aoun, J. and D. Sportiche. 1983. "On the Formal Theory of Government". *The Linguistic Review* 2.211-236.

Bates, E. 1976. *Language and Context*. New York: Academic Press.

Berwick, R. 1985. *The Acquisition of Syntactic Knowledge*. Cambridge, Massachusetts: MIT Press.

Bley-vroman, R. 1989. "The Logical Problem of Second Language Learning". *Linguistic Perspectives on Second Language Acquisition* ed. by S.Gass and J.Schachter, 41-72. Cambridge: Cambridge University Press.

Bloom, L. 1970. *Language Development: Form and Function in Emerging Grammars*. Cambridge, Massachusetts: MIT Press.

Bloom, L., K. Lifter, and J. Hafitz. 1980. "Semantics of Verbs and the Development of Verb Inflection in Child Language". *Language* 56.386-412.

Bloom, L., P. Lightbown and L. Hood. 1975. *Structure and Variation in Child Language*. Monographs of the Society for Research in Child Development. 40.

Bloom, P. 1990. "Subjectless Sentences in Child Language". *Linguistic Inquiry* 21.491-504.

Bohannon, J. and L. Stanowicz. 1988. "The issue of negative evidence: adult responses to children's language errors". *Developmental Psychology* 24.684-689

Borer, H. 1983. *Parametric Syntax*. Dordrecht: Foris.

Borer, H. and K. Wexler. 1987. "Maturational Syntax". *Parameter Setting* ed. by T. Roeper and E. Williams, 123-172. Dordrecht: D.Reidel.

Braine, M. 1974. "Length Constraints, Reduction Rules, and holophrastic processes in Children's Word Combinations". *Journal of Verbal Learning and Verbal Behavior* 13.448-461.

# REFERENCES

Brown, R. 1973. *A First Language: The Early Stages.* Cambridge, Massachusetts: Harvard University Press.

Brown, R. and J. Berko. 1960. "Word Association and the Acquisition of Grammar". *Child Development* 31.1-14.

Brown, R. and C. Hanlon. 1970. "Derivational Complexity and the Order of Acquisition in Child Speech". *Cognition and the Development of Language* ed. by J.R. Hayes, 11-54. New York: John Wiley.

Burt, M., H. Dulay, and E. Hernandez-Chavez. 1975. *Bilingual Syntax Measure.* New York: Harcourt, Brace, Jovanovich.

Cancino, H., E. Rosansky and J. Schumann. 1974. "Testing Hypotheses about Second language Acquisition: the copula and negative in three subjects". *Working Papers in Bilingualism* 6.80-96.

Cazden, C., H. Canino, J. Schumann, and E. Rosansky. 1975. *Second Language Acquisition Sequences in Children, Adolescents and Adults.* Final Report submitted to the National Institute of Education, Washington, D.C.

Chomsky, N. 1981. *Lectures on Government and Binding.* Dordrecht: Foris.

Chomsky, N. 1982. *Some Concepts and Consequences of the Theory of Government and Binding.* Cambridge: MIT Press.

Chomsky, N. 1986a. *Knowledge of Language: Its Nature, Origin and Use.* New York: Prager.

Chomsky, N. 1986b. *Barriers.* Cambridge, Massachusetts: MIT Press.

Chomsky, N. 1988. *Language and Problems of Knowledge.* Cambridge, Massachusetts: MIT Press.

Clahsen, H. 1986. "Verb Inflection in German Child Language: Acquisition of Agreement Marking and the Functions they encode". *Linguistics* 24.79-121.

Clahsen, H. and P. Muysken. 1986. "The Availability of Universal Grammar to adult and Child Learners: A Study of the Acquisition of German Word Order". *Second Language Research* 2.93-119.

Cook, V.J. 1988. *Chomsky's Universal Grammar: An Introduction.* Oxford: Basil Blackwell.

Cox, D. 1970. *The Analysis of Binary Data.* London: Methuen and Co.

Curtiss, A. 1977. *Genie: A Linguistic Study of a Modern Day "Wild Child".* New York: Academic Press.

Dato, D. 1970. *American Children's Acquisition of Spanish Syntax in the Madrid Environment.* Final report, Project No. 3036, Contract No. O.E.C. 2-7-002 637), US Department of Health Education and Welfare.

Deprez, V. and A. Pierce. 1993. "Negation and Functional Projections in Early Grammar". *Linguistic Inquiry* 24.25-68.

Draper, N. and H. Smith. 1981. *Applied Regression Analysis.* New York: John Wiley.

# REFERENCES

Dulay, H. and M.Burt. 1974. "Natural Sequences in Child Second Language Acquisition." *Language Learning* 24.37-53.

Duranti, A. 1984. "The Social Meaning of Subject Pronouns in Italian conversation". *Text* 4.277-311.

Enc, M. 1986. "Topic switching and pronominal subjects in Turkish". *Studies in Turkish Liinguistics* ed. by D. Slobin and K. Zimmer, 195-208. Amsterdam: John Benjamins.Eubank, L. 1991. *Point Counterpoint: Universal Grammar in the Second Language.* Amsterdam: John Benjamins.

Eubank, L. 1991. *Point Counterpoint: Universal Grammar in the Second Language.* Amsterdam:John Benjamins.

Felix, S. 1976. "Linguistische Untersuchungen zum Englisch-Deutschen Zweitsprachernerwerb unter Natürlichen Bedingungen". Habitalationsschrift, Kiel University. Arbeitspapiere zum Spracherwerb Nr.18.Published 1978, München.

Felix, S. 1980. "Interference, Interlanguage and Related Issues". *Second Language Development* ed. by S.Felix, 93-108.Tubingen: Gunter Narr.

Felix, S. 1985. "More Evidence on Competing Cognitive Systems". *Second Language Research* 1.47-72.

Felix, S. 1991. "The Accessibility of Universal Grammar in Second language Acquisition". *Point Counterpoint: Universal Grammar in the Second Language* ed. by L. Eubank, 89-104. Amsterdam: John Benjamins.

Fleiss, J.L. 1981. *Statistical Methods for Rates and Proportions.* New York: John Wiley.

Flynn, S. 1987. *A Parameter-Setting Model of L2 Acquisition.* Dordrecht: Reidel.

Flynn, S. and S. Manuel. 1991. "Age Dependent Effects in Language Acquisition: An Evaluation of "Critical Period" Hypotheses". *Point Counterpoint: Universal Grammar in the Second Language* ed. by L. Eubank, 117-147. Amsterdam: John Benjamins.

Flynn, S. and W. O'Neil, eds. 1988. *Linguistic Theory in Second Language Acquisition.* Dordrecht: Kluwer.

Frazier, L. and J. de Villiers, eds. 1990. *Language Processing and Language Acquisition.* Dordrecht: Kluwer Academic Publishers.

Gass, S. 1988. "Integrating Research Areas: A Framework for Second Language Studies". *Applied Linguistics* 9.198-218.

Gass, S. 1993. "Second Language Acquisition: Past, Present and Future". *Second Language Research* 9.99-117.

Gass, S. and J. Ard. 1980. "L2 data: their Relevance for Language Universals". *TESOL Quarterly* 15.443-452.

Gass, S. and U. Lakshmanan. 1991. "Accounting for Interlanguage Subject Pronouns". *Second Language Research* 7.181-203.

Gass, S. and J. Schachter, eds. 1989. *Linguistic Perspectives on Second Language Acquisition*. Cambridge: Cambridge University Press.

Gerbault, J. 1978. *The Acquisition of English by a Five-Year-Old French Speaker*. Unpublished M.A. Thesis, University of California at Los Angeles.

Gerken, L. 1991. "The Metrical Basis for Children's Subjectless Sentences". *Journal of Memory and Language* 30.431-451.

Geschwind, N. 1980. "Some Comments on the Neurology of Language". *Biological Studies of Mental Processes* ed. by D. Caplan, 301-319. Cambridge, Massachusetts: MIT Press.

Gilligan, F. 1987. *A Cross-Linguistic Approach to the Pro-drop Parameter*. Doctoral Dissertation, University of Southern California, Los Angeles.

Gleitman, L. and E. Wanner. 1982. "Language Acquisition: The State of the State of the Art". *Language Acquisition: The State of the Art* ed. by E. Wanner and L. Gleitman, 3-50. Cambridge: Cambridge University Press.

Gleitman, L. 1986. "Biological Preprogramming for Language Learning". *The Brain, Cognition, and Education* ed. by S. Freidman, K. Kllivington and R. Peterson, 119-149. Orlando: Academic Press.

Grondin, N. and L. White. 1993. "Functional Categories in Child L2 Acquisition of French". *McGill Working Papers in Linguistics* 9.121-145.

Gruber, J. 1967. "Topicalization in Child Language". *Foundations of Language* 3.37-65.

Guilfoyle, E. 1984. "The Acquisition of Tense and the Emergence of Lexical Subjects". *The McGill Working papers in Linguistics* 2.20-30.

Guilfoyle, E. and M. Noonan. 1992. "Functional Categories and Language Acquisition". *Canadian Journal of Linguistics* 37.241-272.

Hakuta, K. 1974. "Prefabricated Patterns and the Emergence of Structure in Second Language Acquisition". *Language Learning* 24.287-297.

Hakuta, K. 1975. *Becoming Bilingual at the Age of Five: The Story of Uguisu*. Unpublished Honors Thesis, Harvard University.

Hakuta, K. 1976. "A Case Study of a Japanese Child Learning English as a Second Language". *Language Learning* 26.321-351.

Hayes, J.R. 1970. *Cognition and the Development of Language*. New York: John Wiley.

Hays, W.L. 1963. *Statistics for Psychologists*. New York: Holt, Rinehart and Winston.

Hilles, S. 1986. "Interlanguage and the Pro-drop Parameter". *Second Language Research* 2.33-52.

Hilles, S. 1989. *Access to UG in Second Language Acquisition*. Doctoral dissertation, University of California, Los Angeles.

# 152 REFERENCES

Hilles, S. 1991. "Access to Universal Grammar in Second Language Acquisition". *Point Counterpoint: Universal Grammar in the Second Language* ed. by L. Eubank, 305-338. Amsterdam: John Benjamins.

Hirsch-Pasek, K., Treiman, R. and Schneiderman, M. 1984. "Brown and Hanlon Revisited: Mothers' Sensitivity to Ungrammatical Forms". *Journal of Child Language* 11.81-88.

Hochberg, J.G. 1986. "Functional Compensation for /s/ deletion in Puerto Rican Spanish". *Language* 62.609-621.

Hornstein, N. and D. Lightfoot eds 1981. *Explanation in Linguistics: The Logical Problem of Language Acquisition*. London: Longman.

Huang, J. 1970. *A Chinese Child's Acquisition of English Syntax*. Unpublished Master's thesis, University of California, Los Angeles.

Huang, C.T.J. 1982. *Between Syntax and Logical Form: A Case Study in Chinese*. Doctoral dissertation, MIT, Cambridge, Massachusetts.

Huang, C.T.J. 1984. "On the Distribution and Reference of Empty Pronouns". *Linguistic Inquiry* 15.531-574.

Hulk, A. 1987. "L'Acquisition du Français et le parametre pro-drop". *Études de Linguistique Française* ed. by B. Kamers-Manhe, 53-61. Amsterdam: Rodopi.

Hyams, N. 1983. *The Acquisition of Parameterized Grammars*. Doctoral Dissertation, City University of New York.

Hyams, N. 1986. *Language Acquisition and the Theory of Parameters*. Dordrecht: Reidel.

Hyams, N. 1992. "A Reanalysis of Null Subjects in Child Language". *Theoretical Issues in Language Acquisition* ed. by J. Weissenborn, H.Goodluck and T.Roeper, 249-269. Hillsdale, New Jersey: Lawrence Erlbaum.

Hyams, N. and Safir, K. 1991. "Evidence, Analogy and Passive Knowledge: Comments on Lakshmanan". *Point Counterpoint: Universal Grammar in the Second Language* ed. by L. Eubank, 411-418. Amsterdam: John Benjamins.

Hyams, N. and Wexler, K. 1993. "On the Grammatical Basis of Null Subjects in Child Language". *Linguistic Inquiry* 24.421-460.

Ilyin, D. 1972. *Ilyin Oral Interview*. Rowley: Newbury House.

Jackendoff, R. 1977. *X-syntax: A Study of Phrase Structure*. Cambridge, Massachusetts: MIT Press.

Jaeggli, O. 1980. *On Some Phonologically Null Elements in Syntax*. Doctoral Dissertation, Massachusetts Institute of Technology, Cambridge, Massachusetts.

Jaeggli, O. 1982. *Topics in Romance Syntax*. Dordrecht: Foris Publications.

Jaeggli, O. and N.Hyams. 1988. "Morphological Uniformity and the Setting of the Null Subject Parameter". *Proceedings of NELS* 18.238-253. GLSA, University of Massachusetts, Amherst.

Jaeggli, O. and K. Safir. 1989. "The Null Subject Parameter and Parametric Theory". *The Null Subject Parameter* ed. by O.Jaeggli and K. Safir. 1-44, Dordrecht: D. Reidel.

Johnson, J. and E. Newport. 1989. "Critical Period Effects in Second Language Learning: The Influence of Maturational State on the Acquisition of English as a Second Language". *Cognitive Psychology* 21. 60-99.

Kaper, W. 1976. "Pronominal Case Errors". *Journal of Child Language* 3.439-441.

Keil, F. 1982. "Constraints on Knowledge and Cognitive Development". *Psychological Review* 88.197-227.

Krashen, S., M. Long and R. Scarcella. 1979. "Age, Rate, and Eventual Attainment in Second Language Acquisition". *TESOL Quarterly* 11.338-341.

Kuriya, Y. 1985. *Ellipsis in Japanese.* ms., University of Michigan, Ann Arbor

Lakshmanan, U. 1986. "The Role of Parametric Variation in Adult Second Language Acquisition: A Study of the Pro-drop Parameter". *Papers in Applied Linguistics-Michigan* 2.97-118.

Lakshmanan, U. 1989. *Accessibility to Universal Grammar in Child Second Language Acquisition.* Doctoral dissertation, University of Michigan, Ann Arbor.

Lakshmanan, U. 1991. "Morphological Uniformity and Null-Subjects in Child Second Language Acquisition". *Point Counterpoint: Universal Grammar in the Second Language* ed. by L. Eubank, 389-411. Amsterdam: John Benjamins.

Lakshmanan, U. 1993/1994. "The Boy for the Cookie--Some Evidence for the non-violation of the Case Filter in Child Second Language Acquisition". *Language Acquisition* 3, 55-91.

Lakshmanan, U. and L. Selinker. 1994. "The Status of CP and the Tensed Complementizer *that* in the developing L2 grammars of English". *Second Language Research* 10. 24-48.

Larsen-Freeman, D. 1976. "An Explanation for the Morpheme Acquisition Order of Second Language Learners". *Language Learning* 26.125-134.

Larsen-Freeman, D. and M. Long. 1991. *An Introduction to Second Language Acquisition Research.* London: Longman.

Lebeaux, D. 1988. *Language Acquisition and the Form of the Grammar.* Ph.D. Dissertation, University of Massachusetts, Amherst.

Lenneberg, E. 1967. *Biological Foundations of Language.* New York: Wiley.

# REFERENCES

Liceras, J.M. 1988. "Syntax and Stylistics: More on the Pro-Drop Parameter". *Learnability and Second Languages: A Book of Readings.* ed. by Pankhurst, J., M. Sharwood-smith and P. van Buren, 71-93. Dordrecht: Foris

Lightbown, P. and L.White. 1988. The Influence of Linguistic Theories on Language Acquisition Research. *Language Learning* 37.483-510.

Lillo-Martin, D. 1991. *Universal Grammar and American Sign Language.* Dordrecht: Kluwer Academic Publishers.

Long, M. 1990. "Maturational Constraints on Language Development". *Studies in Second Language Acquisition* 12. 251-285.

Lust, B, ed. 1986. *Studies in the Acquisition of Anaphora: Defining the Constraints, Vol. 1.* Dordrecht : Reidel.

Lust, B, ed. 1988. *Studies in the Acquisition of Anaphora: Applying the Constraints, Vol. 2.* Dordrecht: Reidel.

Manzini, R. and Wexler, K. 1987. "Parameters, Binding Theory and Learnability". *Linguistic Inquiry* 18.413-444.

Mazuka, R., B. Lust, T. Wakayama and W. Snyder. 1986. "Distinguishing Effects of Parameters in Early Syntax Acquisition: A Cross-linguistic Study of Japanese and English". *Papers and Reports on Child Language Development* 25.73-82.

Mazurkewich, I. 1984. "The Acquisition of the Dative Alternation by Second Language Learners and Linguistic Theory". *Language Learning* 34.91-109.

McDaniel, D. and C.Mckee 1992. "Which Children Did They Show Obey Strong Crossover?". *Island Constraints* ed. by H. Goodluck and M.Rochemont. Dordrecht: Kluwer Academic Publishers.

Meisel, J.M. 1980. "Linguistic Simplification". *Second Language Development. Trends and Issues* ed. by S. Felix, 13-40. Tubingen: Gunter Narr.

Milon, J. 1974. "The Development of Negation in English by a Second Language Learner". *TESOL Quarterly* 8.137-143.

Mohanan, K.P. 1983. "Functional and Anaphoric Control". *Linguistic Inquiry.* 14.641-674.

Morgan, J. and L.Travis. 1989. "Limits on Negative Information in Language Input". *Journal of Child Language* 16.531-552.

Nicholas, H. 1981. " 'To be' or not 'to be': Is that Really the Question? Developmental Sequences and the Role of the Copula in the Acquisition of German as a Second Language". Paper Presented at the First European-North American Workshop on Cross-Linguistic Second Language Acquisition Research.

O'Grady, W. 1991. "Language Acquisition and the "Pro-Drop" Phenomenon: A Response to Hilles". *Point Counterpoint: Universal Grammar in the Second Language* ed. by L. Eubank, 339-350. Amsterdam: John Benjamins.

O'Grady, W., A. Peters, and D. Masterson. 1989. "The Transition from Optional to Required Subjects". *Journal of Child Language* 16.513-529.

Peters, A. 1983. *The Units of Language Acquisition.* Cambridge: Cambridge University Press.

Phinney, M. 1987. "The Pro-drop Parameter in Second Language Acquisition". *Parameter Setting* ed. by T. Roeper and E. Williams, 221-238. Dordrecht: D.Reidel.

Pinker, S. 1984. *Language Learnability and Language Development.* Cambridge: Harvard University Press.

Platzack, C. 1985. "The Scandinavian Languages and the Null Subject Parameter". *Natural Language and Linguistic Theory* 5. 377-402.

Poeppel, D. and K. Wexler. 1993. "The Full Competence Hypothesis of Clause Structure in German". *Language* 69.1-33.

Radford, A. 1990. *Syntactic Theory and the Acquisition of English Syntax.* Oxford:Basil Blackwell.

Ravem, R. 1978. "Two Norwegian Children's Acquisition of English Syntax". *Second Language Acquisition: A Book of Readings* ed. by E.Hatch,148-154. Rowley, Massachusetts: Newbury House.

Rizzi, L. 1982. *Issues in Italian Syntax.* Dordrecht: Foris Publications.

Roberge,Y. 1986. "On Doubling and Null Argument Languages". *Proceedings of NELS* 16.388-402.

Roeper, T. 1978. "Linguistic Universals and the Acquisition of Gerunds". *Papers in the Structure and Development of Child Language 4.* ed. by H. Goodluck and L. Solan, 1-36. University of Massachussetts Occasional Papers in Linguistics.

Roeper, T. 1981. "On the Deductive Model and the Acquisition of Productive Morphology". *The Logical Problem of Language Acquisition* ed. by C.L. Baker and J. McCarthy, 129-164. Cambridge, Massachusetts: MIT Press.

Roeper, T. 1986. "How Children Acquire Bound Variables". *Studies in the Acquisition of Anaphora: Defining the Constraints, Vol. 1.* ed. by B. Lust, 191-202. Dordrecht: Reidel.

Roeper, T., M.Rooth, L. Mallis, and S. Akiyama. 1984. "The Problem of Empty Categories and Bound Variables in Language Acquisition". ms., University of Massachusetts, Amherst.

Roeper, T. and J. Weissenborn. 1990. "How to Make Parameters Work: Comments on Valian." *Language Processing and Language Acquisition* ed. by L. Frazier and J. de Villiers, 147-163. Dordrecht: Kluwer Academic Publishers.

Roeper, T. and E. Williams, eds. 1987. *Parameter Setting.* Dordrecht: Reidel.

Ross, J. R. 1982. "Pronoun Deleting Processes in German." Paper presented at the annual meeting of the Linguistic Society of America, San Diego, California.

Rutherford, W. 1986. "Grammatical Theory and L2 Acquisition: a Brief overview". *Second Language Research* 2.1-15.

Safir, K. 1982. *Syntactic Chains and the Definiteness Effect*. Doctoral dissertaion, Massachusetts Institute of Technology, Cambridge, Massachusetts.

Safir, K. 1985. *Syntactic Chains*. Cambridge University Press.

Schachter, J. 1984. "A Universal Input Condition". *Language Universals and Second Language Acquisition*. ed. by W. Rutherford, 167-184. Amsterdam: John Benjamins.

Schachter, J. 1990. "On the Issue of Completeness in Second Language Acquisition". *Second Language Research* 6. 93-124.

Schwartz, B. (1987). *The Modular Basis of Second Language Acquisition*. Unpublished Doctoral Dissertation, University of Southern California, Los Angeles.

Selinker, L. 1972. "Interlanguage". *International Review of Applied Linguistics* 10.209-230.

Selinker, L., M. Swain and G. Dumas. 1975. "The Interlanguage Hypothesis Extended to Children". *Language Learning* 25.139-152.

Sharwood Smith, M. 1988. "L2 Acquisition: Logical Problems and Empirical Solutions". *Learnability and Second Languages: A Book of Readings* ed. by Pankhurst, J., M. Sharwood Smith and P. van Buren, 9-35. Dordrecht: Foris.

Shatz, M. and K. Ebeling. 1991. "Patterns of Language Learning-Related Behaviors in Two-year-olds: Evidence for Self-Help in Acquiring Grammar". *Journal of Child Language* 18.295-313.

Slobin, D. 1967. "Imitation and Grammatical Development in Children". *Contemporary Issues in Developmental Psychology* ed. by N.S. Endler, L.R. Boulter and H. Osser, 437-443. New York: Holt.

Stowell, T. 1981. *Origins of Phrase Structure*. Doctoral Dissertation, Massachusetts Institute of Technology, Cambridge, Massachusetts.

Taraldsen, T. 1978. *On NIC, Vacuous Application and the That-trace Filter*. Mimeographed M.I.T. ms., Distributed by the Indiana University Linguistics Club, Bloomington, Indiana.

Thomas, M. 1989. "The Interpretation of English Reflexive Pronouns by Non-Native Speakers". *Studies in Second Language Acquisition* 11.281-303.

Tiphine, U. 1983. *The Acquisition of English Statements and Interrogatives by French-Speaking Children*. Doctoral dissertation, University of Kiel.

Tsao, F. 1977. *A Functional Study of Topic in Chinese: A First Step toward Discourse Analysis*. Doctoral dissertation, University of Southern California, Los Angeles.

Valian, V. 1990. "Logical and Psychological Constraints on the Acquisition of Syntax". *Language Processing and Language Acquisition* ed. by L. Frazier and J. de Villiers, 119-146. Dordrecht: Kluwer Academic Publishers.

Valian, V. 1991. "Syntactic Subjects in the Early Speech of American and Italian Children". *Cognition* 40. 21-81.

Valian, V. 1992. "Categories of First Syntax: Be, Be+ing, and Nothingness". *The Acquisition of Verb Placement: Functional Categories and V2 Phenomena in Language Acquisition* ed. by J. Meisel, 401-422. Dordrecht: Kluwer Academic Publishers.

Van Buren, P. 1988. "Some Remarks on the Subset Principle in Second Language Acquisition". *Second Language Research* 4.33-40.

Wang, Q., D. Lillo-Martin, C. Best and A. Levitt. 1992. "Null Subjects and Objects in the Acquisition of Chinese." *Language Acquisition* 2.221-254.

Weinberg, A. 1987. "Comments on Borer and Wexler." *Parameter Setting* ed. by T. Roeper and E. Williams, 173-188. Dordrecht: Reidel.

Weissenborn, J. 1992. "Null Subjects in Early Grammars: Implications for Parameter Setting Theories". *Theoretical Issues in Language Acquisition* ed. by J. Weissenborn, H.Goodluck and T.Roeper, 269-301. Hillsdale, New Jersey: Lawrence Erlbaum.

Weissenborn, J., H.Goodluck and T.Roeper, eds. 1992. *Theoretical Issues in Language Acquisition*. Hillsdale, New Jersey: Lawrence Erlbaum.

Weist, R. and K.Witkowska-Stadnik. 1985. "Basic Relations in Child Language and the Word Order Myth". Unpublished ms., SUNY/ Fredonia and Adam Mickiewicz University.

White, L. 1982. *Grammatical Theory and Language Acquisition*. Dordrecht: Foris.

White, L. 1985a. "The Acquisition of Parameterized Grammars: Subjacency in Second Language Acquisition". *Second Language Research* 1.No 1-117.

White, L. 1985b. "The Pro-drop Parameter in Adult Second language Acquisition". *Language Learning* 35.47-62.

White, L. 1985c. "Is There a "Logical Problem" of Second language Acquisition?". *TESL Canada Journal* 2.29-41.

White, L. 1989. *Universal Grammar and Second Language Acquisition*. Amsterdam: John Benjamins.

White, L. 1990/1991. "The Verb Movement Parameter in Second Language Acquisition". *Language Acquisition* 1.337-360.

White, L. 1992. "Long and Short Verb Movement in Second Language Acquisition". *Canadian Journal of Linguistics* 37.273-286.

Wode, H. 1978. "Developmental Sequences in Naturalistic L2 Acquisition". *Second Language Acquisition: A Book of Readings* ed. by E.Hatch, 101-117. Rowley, Massachusetts: Newbury House.

Wong-Fillmore, Lily. 1976. *The Second Time Around: Cognitive and Social Strategies in Second Language Acquisition*. Doctoral Dissertation, Stanford University, Stanford.

Zobl, H. 1984. "Uniformity and Source-language Variation across Developmental continua". *Language Universals and Second Language Acquisition*. ed. by W. Rutherford, 185-219.Amsterdam: John Benjamins.

Zobl, H. 1988. "Configurationality and the Subset Principle: The Acquisition of V' by Japanese Learners of English." *Learnability and Second Languages: A Book of Readings* ed. by Pankhurst, J., M. Sharwood-smith and P. van Buren, 116-131. Dordrecht: Foris.

# Index

access to Universal Grammar 16-18, 21-23, 61, 141
active knowledge 69, 70, 124
AG/PRO parameter 33, 34, 68
AGR 30-33, 42, 43, 50, 55, 64
American Sign Language(ASL) 41, 47
apperceived input 140
Arabic 68
AUX 34, 49, 50, 68
Bengali 41
c-command 35, 43, 44, 58, 128
case
    accusative 64, 69
    nominative 31, 32, 42
Case Filter 49, 146
Chinese 1, 7, 8, 15, 25, 27, 30, 35-37, 39, 40, 43, 44, 47, 49, 51, 52, 54, 56-58, 63, 64, 66, 127-129, 136
complementizer 25, 29
contradictory data 10, 59, 66, 126, 134, 145
creative construction hypothesis 18
critical period 9, 14-17
D-structure 6, 7
Developmental Problem 8, 9, 20
direct access 21, 22, 60, 64, 141
Discourse oriented
    Parameter (DOP) 58, 59, 128, 129, 143-145

Empty Category Principle(ECP) 32
English 1, 2, 4, 7-10, 16, 23-25, 27, 30-34, 36, 39-41, 43, 45, 47-75, 77-80, 83, 90, 92, 120-134, 136-141, 143-147
equivalence strategy 137, 141
expletive subjects 32, 40, 46, 47, 49, 50, 85
Extended Projection Principle 30, 31
French 1, 2, 23, 27, 30, 32, 39, 40, 43, 45, 46, 48, 53, 64, 68, 69, 73, 75, 99, 120, 135, 136, 140, 144, 146
functional categories 25, 29, 49, 146
German 28, 30, 37, 40, 41, 43, 46, 48, 67
Government 31
Government and Binding theory (GB) 1, 3, 5, 6, 27, 28, 31, 34, 42, 45
Icelandic 43
Identification 28, 37, 41-45, 50, 51, 57, 67, 127, 129, 136
    agreement 42, 44, 51, 127
    c-commanding 43, 44

# INDEX

indirect access 18, 21, 22, 60, 141
individual differences 19, 119, 138, 139
INFL 27-34, 42-45, 49, 67, 146
Interlanguage(IL) 2, 9, 17, 18, 21, 22, 24, 60-65, 67, 68, 71-73, 77, 82-86, 88, 89, 92-96, 98-102, 105-112, 114-121, 125, 127, 129, 130-132, 134, 136, 137, 138-142, 144-146
instantaneous model of language acquisition 7, 9
intake 10
Italian 1, 27, 30, 31, 33, 34, 38, 39, 42-45, 47, 49, 50, 52, 54-56, 58, 64, 66-68, 122, 127-129
Japanese 1, 2, 7, 27, 30, 35-37, 39, 43, 44, 64, 68, 73, 75, 118, 127, 128, 136, 137, 140, 144, 145, 147
Korean 27
language acquisition
   first language acquisition 5, 8, 9, 11, 14, 15, 17, 20, 47, 51, 76, 146
   second language acquisition (SLA) 1, 5, 8, 11, 12, 14, 16, 18, 19, 28, 45, 59, 63, 68, 71, 73, 101, 127, 129, 142, 143, 145-147
     adult L2 12, 15, 16, 18, 19, 23, 68, 139, 147
     child L2 12, 15, 19-22, 67, 127, 129, 141, 143, 144-146

learnability 2, 13, 21, 52, 67, 122, 125, 126
learning procedure 8, 13, 14, 16-17
lexical categories 29, 32
Logical Form(LF) 6, 7, 25
Logical Problem of Language Acquisition 3, 5, 20
Malayalam 30, 35
maturation factors 10-12, 14, 16, 20
maximal projection 29, 31, 146
morphological uniformity 1, 2, 28, 37, 41, 42, 50, 54, 56, 61, 71, 122
Move α 6-9
negative evidence 3, 5, 13, 24, 25
no access 22, 60, 61, 141, 142
non-equivalence strategy 137, 139, 145
null objects 58, 128, 136, 140
Null Pronoun Parameter 58, 59, 128, 129, 143, 144, 145
Null Subject Parameter 10, 27
null subjects 1, 2, 28, 31, 34, 37, 38, 40-46, 48, 50, 51, 56-58, 60-67, 69-72, 77, 78, 80-121, 123, 124, 126-130, 132, 134, 136-140, 142, 144, 145
  in embedded clauses 43, 45, 57-59, 67, 126-128, 130-134, 136, 138, 143, 145, 147
  in *is* contexts 71, 72, 78, 82, 92-101, 119, 122, 130, 132, 136, 138, 139, 142-145
  in *non-is* contexts 71, 78, 79, 93, 97-101, 103

parameter setting 9, 10, 12, 13, 16, 22, 48, 49, 52, 59, 61, 101, 120, 123, 125, 126, 127, 129, 130, 139, 145
   resetting 18, 21, 22, 60, 61, 68, 128, 129, 141, 143, 144
parameters 7-10, 13, 16-18, 21, 25, 128, 144, 145
passive knowledge 69, 70, 124
perceptual factors 2, 12, 101, 119, 127, 129, 137, 138, 142-144
performance factors 23, 48, 59, 129, 134
Phonetic Form(PF) 6
positive evidence 7-9, 13, 14, 17, 21, 22, 52, 55, 58, 60, 122, 126, 128, 129, 139, 143, 144
Principles and Parameters theory 3, 7-9, 21
PRO 28, 31-37, 42-44, 49, 50, 57, 58, 68, 128
*pro* 32, 33, 35-37, 43, 44, 58, 59
pro-drop 10, 27, 28, 31-35, 41, 45, 46, 49, 50, 61, 68, 69, 125-126, 147
   non-pro-drop languages 27, 32, 34, 39, 49, 50, 99, 125
pro-drop parameter 28, 34, 49, 68, 126; *see also* null subject parameter
proper government 32
referential Subjects 28, 32, 43, 46, 49, 67, 127, 136
rich agreement 31, 33, 34, 37, 42, 44, 58, 128, 129, 143

S-structure 6
saliency 124, 137
sentence oriented 36, 43, 64, 141
silent period 69, 133, 139, 140, 141
Spanish 1, 2, 23, 27, 30-34, 38-40, 42-45, 49, 50, 54, 62-65, 67-69, 73-74, 76, 78, 85, 120, 122, 129, 130, 132-134, 139, 140, 143-145, 147
Structure dependency 3, 11
subject object asymmetry 128
Subset Principle 13, 14, 52, 54, 55, 66, 122
tense 29-31, 38-40, 42, 43, 55, 65, 67, 79, 80, 81, 102, 125
thematic roles 32, 42
Theta Criterion 41
topic
   discourse topic 43-44, 58, 128
   empty topic 37
   null topic 43, 57
   topic chaining 37, 43, 51, 63, 64, 66, 127, 128
   zero topic 37
topic-comment structures 56, 137
Transfer 18, 22, 60-63, 68, 130, 139, 140, 141
triggering data 8-11, 13, 14, 16, 17, 68, 145; *see also* unique trigger
Turkish 46
unique trigger 10, 59, 126, 127, 131, 133, 145, 147
Universal Grammar(UG) 1, 2, 5-14, 16, 17, 28, 45, 49, 59-

62, 64, 66, 119, 137, 139, 141-143
ungrammatical input 10, 133, 134
V-S order in declaratives 68
variables 36, 37, 42, 57, 58, 100, 128
verb agreement 27-29, 31, 33, 34, 37, 42-44, 50, 58, 64, 65, 67, 79-81, 102, 125,127, 144
verb inflections 1, 2, 23, 50, 51, 53, 54, 61-63, 65, 71, 72, 77, 80, 82, 86, 87, 90, 92, 98, 102, 104, 108, 110, 114, 118, 120, 122, 123-125, 128, 144
VP length 48
X-bar theory 29, 34

In the series LANGUAGE ACQUISITION AND LANGUAGE DISORDERS (LALD) the following titles have been published thus far:

1. WHITE, Lydia: *Universal Grammar Second Language Acquisition.* Amsterdam/Philadelphia, 1989.
2. HUEBNER, Thom and Charles A. FERGUSON (eds): *Crosscurrents in Second Language Acquisition and Linguistic Theories.* Amsterdam/Philadelphia, 1991.
3. EUBANK, Lynn (ed.): *Point-Counter-Point. Universal Grammar and Second Language Acquisition.* Amsterdam/Philadelphia, 1991.
4. ECKMAN, Fred R. (ed.): *Confluence. Linguistics, L2 acquisition and speech pathology.* Amsterdam/Philadelphia, 1993.
5. GASS, Susan and Larry SELINKER (eds): *Language Transfer in Language Learning.* Amsterdam/Philadelphia, 1992.
6. THOMAS, Margaret: *Knowledge of Reflexives in a Second Language.* Amsterdam/Philadelphia, 1993.
7. MEISEL, Juergen M. (ed.): *Bilingual First Language Acquisition.* Amsterdam/Philadelphia, n.y.p.
8. HOEKSTRA, Teun and Bonnie D. SCHWARTZ (eds): *Language Acquisition Studies in Generative Grammar: Papers in honor of Kenneth Wexler from the 1991 GLOW workshops.* Amsterdam/Philadelphia, 1994.
9. ADONE, Dany: *The Acquisition of Mauritian Creole.* Amsterdam/Philadelphia, 1994.
10. LAKSHMANAN, Usha: *Universal Grammar in Child Second Language Acquisition: Null subjects and morphological uniformity.* Amsterdam/Philadelphia, 1994.